IMAGES
of America

HAGERSTOWN IN THE CIVIL WAR

Hagerstown is known for its longstanding symbol Little Heiskell, a weather vane ornament in the form of a German soldier that stood atop Hagerstown City Hall from the early 1800s until the building was demolished and replaced with the current city hall in 1939. Local legend states that the hole near his arm was made by a Confederate soldier who took a potshot at him during the Civil War. When city hall was rebuilt, a replica took its place, and Little Heiskell was retired to exhibit at the Jonathan Hager House Museum in City Park. (Western Maryland Room, Washington County Free Library.)

ON THE COVER. This is North Potomac Street viewed from Public Square in 1867. The building with the clock tower is the town hall, now the site of city hall. (Washington County Historical Society.)

IMAGES
of America

HAGERSTOWN IN THE CIVIL WAR

Stephen R. Bockmiller

ARCADIA
PUBLISHING

Published by Arcadia Publishing
Charleston, South Carolina

Printed in the United States of America

Library of Congress Control Number: 2010931209

For all general information, please contact Arcadia Publishing:
Telephone 843-853-2070
Fax 843-853-0044
E-mail sales@arcadiapublishing.com
For customer service and orders:
Toll-Free 1-888-313-2665

Visit us on the Internet at www.arcadiapublishing.com

Dedicated to every Civil War veteran, North and South, who lived in Hagerstown before, during, or after the Civil War, and to Hagerstown's 4,500 wartime residents. Americans all.

Contents

Acknowledgments   6

Introduction   7

1.   A Sleepy County Seat
     Antebellum Hagerstown   9

2.   Off to War and Soldiers Come to Hagerstown
     1860–1862   33

3.   War in the Streets
     1863   57

4.   Ransom, Redemption, Peace, and Tragedy
     1864–1865   89

5.   Recovery, Reunion, and Remembrance
     Hagerstown After the War   103

ACKNOWLEDGMENTS

The City of Hagerstown is grateful to the following persons and organizations whose cooperation and support were essential in preparing this work: the Hagerstown/Washington County Convention and Visitors Bureau, Thomas B. Riford, president and chief executive officer; the Heart of the Civil War Heritage Area, Elizabeth Scott Shatto, director; the Washington County Historical Society, Linda Irvin-Craig, director, and Cathy Landsman, registrar; the Western Maryland Room of the Washington County Free Library, John Frye, manager; the *Maryland Cracker Barrel* magazine, Frank and Suzanne Woodring, publishers; Clif Hyatt, the U.S. Army Heritage and Education Center, Carlisle, Pennsylvania; the Library of Congress; the U.S. Senate Historical Office; the Town of Sandy Creek, New York, Charlene Cole, historian; the Georges Creek Historical Society, Lonaconing, Maryland; the National Park Service; Capt. Justin Mayhue of the Hagerstown Fire Department; Western Enterprise Fire Company; John Gartrell, *Baltimore Afro-American* newspaper; Kathleen A. Maher, Hagerstown city planning director; Doug Bast, Boonsboro Museum of History; Stacks Rare Coins, New York, New York; the Margurite Doleman Museum Collection, Hagerstown, Maryland; Lt. Margaret Kline, Hagerstown Police Department (retired); Cynthia Blackstock; William Theriault; Daniel C. Toomey; Joe Bloom; Ted Alexander; Dorothy Smith; Lawrence J. Bopp; Frederick D. Shroyer; Dr. Thomas E. Clemens; Ellen DiBiase; Lewis Mountcastle; Robert Figenshu; Bradley Forbush; Frances Lowrey Brasher; Donald Beagle; Susan Howe; Michael Pekosky; Dr. Mark Bond; Timothy R. Snyder; Charles Mobley; Dennis Easterday; Roger Keller; Dr. Paula Reed; Richard E. Clem; Stephen Donches; Richard Armstrong; Ben Hawley; Greg French; Dave Mark; the American Antiquarian Society, Worcester, Massachusetts; Jim Wolfson; Historical Image Bank; and the West Virginia State Archives. The author also wishes to extend a very special thank-you to his wife, Stefania, and daughter Sarah, who tolerated the overtime and extensive at-home research that he devoted to making this project possible.

All images are credited to their owner or custodian. Images in the collection of the Western Maryland Room, Washington County Free Library are denoted by WMR-WCFL. Images in the collection of the Washington County Historical Society are denoted by WCHS. Images in the collections of the U.S. Army Heritage and Education Center are denoted with USAMHI, followed by special collection references.

The author's acquisition of images has been financed in part by a grant from the Hagerstown–Washington County Convention and Visitors Bureau and by a grant from the Heart of the Civil War Heritage Area, with funds from the Maryland Heritage Areas Authority, an agency of the State of Maryland. The contents and opinions contained here, however, do not necessarily reflect the views or policies of the Maryland Heritage Areas Authority.

INTRODUCTION

Washington County has a rich Civil War history. With Antietam National Battlefield, South Mountain Battlefield State Park, Harpers Ferry National Historical Park, and other sites within the county, there is no shortage of stories to tell. Near such prominent historical sites in the area, Hagerstown is often overlooked when the story of Washington County in the Civil War is considered, yet a myriad of human dramas occurred in "the Hub City" in the years leading up to, during, and after the war that forever impacted the participants and left their marks on the community.

Originally named Elizabeth Town after the wife of its founder, Hagerstown was officially established in 1762 by Jonathan Hager. But a settlement had been located on the site as far back as the 1730s. When Washington County was formed from Frederick County in 1776, it consisted of all of Maryland west of South Mountain and Hager's Town was selected as the county seat. The vastness of the county lasted until 1789, when Allegany County was formed. The community officially adopted its current name of Hagerstown after the War of 1812.

The population of Hagerstown at the outset of the Civil War was approximately 4,500 people. Of these, 494 were "free persons of color," 31 of whom were property owners. Due to its predominantly German heritage and the nature of agriculture in the region, Washington County had relatively few slaves compared to other parts of Maryland. The number of slaves in the city is estimated at a few hundred. Regardless of the general objection to and minimal need for slave labor, the community turned out in the presidential election of 1860 to support the Southern Democrat John C. Breckinridge and the Constitutional Union Party candidate John Bell. Republican Abraham Lincoln and Northern Democrat Stephen Douglas received a small percentage of the vote.

At this time, Hagerstown was served by the Franklin Railroad that connected the city to points north, a telegraph, several banks, and a thriving local economic base centered on the agricultural community and manufacturing. The proximity of the Chesapeake and Ohio Canal also helped the economy. A college for women, public and private schools, a lyceum (debating and performance hall), and other institutions formed a cultural base in the community. Catholic, Episcopal, Lutheran, Methodist, Presbyterian, German Reformed, and two African-American churches provided spiritual homes to area Christians. Hagerstown was home to a small but integrated Jewish community as well.

The results of the election showed Hagerstown to be a community in favor of maintaining the Union, while also respecting the constitutional protection of slavery. There appeared to be little appetite for the Republican platform of preventing the spread of slavery into the territories. But once the first guns were fired on Fort Sumter, battle lines were drawn in Hagerstown, with most citizens favoring the preservation of the Union over all other considerations.

A small but vocal pro-Southern element existed in the community. A local doctor, lawyer, and newspaper editor were caught up in the Lincoln administration's roundup of influential pro-Southern Marylanders and were held in military prisons for over a year. When Confederates marched through Hagerstown in 1862, 1863, and 1864, they were met with slightly warmer receptions than the icy stares they received when they marched through Frederick and Middletown. Yet one rebel lamented that if the attitude of the people in this part of Maryland was any indication of the sentiment of all Marylanders, the Confederacy could forget the Old Line State ever joining its cause. Nonetheless a number of Hagerstonians "went South," and some achieved prominent positions in the Confederate military.

After the war, the community had a mixture of former Union veterans and sympathizers interspersed cooperatively with a smaller cadre of former Confederates and Southern sympathizers. This is the citizenry that led Hagerstown through its heyday from 1880 to 1920 and forms the nucleus around which the modern city is built.

This work was inspired by Hagerstown's recent development of four dozen Civil War trail markers, which are located throughout the city. This book is built upon the collection of images that was compiled for that project. It is our hope that you find inspiration from this work to visit our historic areas and learn more of the stories of Hagerstonians and the city itself during the Civil War.

—Stephen R. Bockmiller

City of Hagerstown
1861

John Cook, mayor

City Council
Lewis Wilhide, Ward 1
George H. L. Chrissinger, Ward 2
Charles H. Henson, Ward 3
Richard Sheckels, Ward 4
Ephriam W. Funk, Ward 5

William M. Tice, city clerk

Andrew K. Syester, city attorney

City of Hagerstown
2011

Robert E. Bruchey, II, mayor

City Council (elected at large)
William M. Breichner
Martin E. Brubaker
Forrest Easton
Ashley C. Haywood
Lewis C. Metzner

Donna K. Spickler, city clerk
Bruce J. Zimmerman, city administrator
John H. Urner, LLC and Nairn and Boyer, LLC, city attorneys

One

A Sleepy County Seat
Antebellum Hagerstown

Lucretia Hart was born in Hagerstown in 1781 and moved with her family to Lexington, Kentucky, at age 3. In 1799, she married a young man with much promise. His name was Henry Clay. Clay was a contender for the presidency in three unsuccessful attempts. Had he succeeded, Hagerstown could have boasted of being the home of a first lady. Nonetheless as a senator and secretary of state, Clay, known as "the Great Compromiser," would become a major figure in forging the political environment that led to Civil War. (WMR-WCFL.)

The Hagerstown Charity School was founded in 1815 by the Hagerstown Female Society with the mission of educating the underprivileged children of mothers who had to work due to the loss of their husbands. The Charity School building, which dates to about 1840, is located at the corner of Locust and East Washington Streets. Founded in 1906, the Hagerstown Day Nursery has occupied the site for over a century. (WCHS.)

This historic collage depicts the prominent doctors of Washington County during the Civil War period. They are, from left to right, James B. McKee, Ezra Wise, Dr. Duckett, Charles McKee, Frederick Dorsey Sr., Frederick Dorsey Jr., Claggett Dorsey, Charles G. W. MacGill, Charles MacGill, Samuel Lungren, and Norman Bruce Scott. The MacGills served the Confederacy. (WCHS.)

The Hagerstown Academy was established in 1810 and was located in the middle of what is now the 100 block of South Prospect Street. Used as a military hospital at times during the Civil War, the school was the alma mater of most of Hagerstown's prominent native sons. The building was demolished to extend South Prospect Street to Heyser's Woods (today's City Park). (City of Hagerstown.)

Prof. George Pearson taught at the Hagerstown Academy. The exact dates of his service on the faculty are not known. (WCHS.)

Abram Ryan was born near Hagerstown in 1838 and baptized at St. Mary's Catholic Church. His family later moved to Missouri, and he was ordained a priest in 1860. It appears Ryan served informal stints as a freelance chaplain with Louisiana troops until his brother died of wounds in early 1863. Soon thereafter, he began serving full time as a chaplain. He was at the Battles of Franklin and Nashville in 1864. In the summer of 1865, his poem "The Conquered Banner" appeared in a New York newspaper and gained fame. He founded *The Banner of the South*, a weekly religious and political paper tinged with nostalgia of the Confederate army. For his life's work, Abram Ryan became known as "The Poet-Priest of the Confederacy." (Donald Beagle, Belmont Abbey College.)

St. Mary's started off as a log mission church and was the first Catholic church in Washington County. As the congregation grew, a new brick church was constructed on the northeast corner of West Washington and Walnut Streets in 1818. It has served as the central church for Hagerstown area Catholics for nearly 200 years. This drawing illustrates the appearance of the church during the Civil War years. Around 1870, the building was heavily renovated to create the front foyer and bell tower seen today. (*Maryland Cracker Barrel.*)

Located just south of the city, Fountain Rock was the home of Samuel Ringgold, a U.S. congressman during the War of 1812. He fathered two sons who made great contributions to the American military. Maj. Samuel Ringgold Jr. became known as "The Father of Modern Artillery" for his innovations in the use of cannon as a mobile force on the battlefield. He was killed at the Battle of Palo Alto in the Mexican War. During the Civil War period, the Ringgold house was the home of St. James College. The residence was lost to fire in 1926, but the school continues on the site to this day. (*Maryland Cracker Barrel.*)

FOUNTAIN ROCK.

Capt. Cadwalader Ringgold was born at Fountain Rock in 1802. He entered the navy in 1819 and spent most of his career on missions exploring and charting the islands of the Pacific Ocean. Early in the Civil War, he commanded the USS *Sabine*, where he was credited with rescuing 400 U.S. Marines from a ship sinking off the coast of South Carolina. Ringgold later commanded ships hunting Confederate commerce raiders. He retired in 1868 with the rank of rear admiral. (Library of Congress.)

13

John Ross Key was the grandson of both Samuel Ringgold and Francis Scott Key. Born at Fountain Rock, he was raised by the author of "The Star Spangled Banner" in Georgetown, D.C., after the death of his parents. A natural artist, the younger Key studied in Europe and returned home to find employment as a draftsman with the U.S. Coastal Survey from 1853 to 1856. The Coastal Survey was the forerunner of today's National Oceanic and Atmospheric Administration. He was sketched (shown) by coworker James McNeill Whistler. Both Key and Whistler became famous artists. Whistler became a leading proponent of the "art for art's sake" movement. His painting *Arrangement in Grey and Black: The Artist's Mother*, popularly known as *Whistler's Mother*, is his most recognizable work. Key gained fame as a painter of frontier landscapes, many of which are held in private and museum collections around the nation. During the Civil War, Key was commissioned a second lieutenant in the engineer corps of the Confederate army. (National Oceanic and Atmospheric Administration.)

Hagerstown flourished when the National Road was constructed, using Frederick and Washington Streets as its route through town, and the city became a major stopover for travelers heading west to the frontier or east to the nation's major cities. The Antietam House, a hotel located across Washington Street from the circuit courthouse, was razed in the 1870s to make way for the Hamilton Hotel that still stands to this day. (WMR-WCFL.)

Edward Mealey was a local attorney and businessman who resided in this stone house located across South Jonathan Street (Summit Avenue) from the circuit courthouse. The home was purchased and razed for the construction of the Nicodemus Bank Building. Today the bank building is the home to the Discovery Station Childrens' Museum (WMR-WCFL.)

A "dry bridge" was constructed in the 1830s to carry Prospect Street over West Antietam Street. Taken from the west side of the underpass, this image captures the area looking eastward on West Antietam Street toward what is now Summit Avenue. In the background is St. John's Lutheran Church on South Potomac Street. (WCHS.)

St. John's Lutheran Church was constructed in 1794 and retains much of its original appearance today. It was located on a hill on the southern edge of town. When the Union army reoccupied Hagerstown after the Battle of Gettysburg, Maj. Gen. Oliver Otis Howard used the bell tower to observe troop movements. The cemetery was later relocated. (WCHS.)

Railroad service to Hagerstown opened in 1841. The Franklin Railroad connected the city to Chambersburg, where the Cumberland Valley Railroad (CVRR) connected to Harrisburg. The Franklin Railroad failed in 1844 but was later absorbed into the CVRR. The CVRR engine *Pioneer* served the line between the Hagerstown and Chambersburg before the Civil War. It was retired to accessory use when the troop and supply trains required by the war effort were too large for this engine to pull. In 2010, *Pioneer* was delivered to the Baltimore and Ohio Railroad Museum in Baltimore for restoration and display. This recent photograph shows the *Pioneer* when it was displayed at the National Museum of Industrial History in Bethlehem, Pennsylvania. (Stephen Donches.)

The Franklin Railroad entered town from the north on Walnut Street and terminated at Washington Street. The first depot was located diagonally across the intersection from the church (to the left of this photograph). The 1860s-era CVRR depot (above) was the second structure to serve this purpose. It was located directly across Washington Street from St. Mary's Catholic Church. This building was replaced in the 1880s by a large Victorian railroad station. This image was taken in the early 1870s after St. Mary's was renovated to its current appearance. (Georges Creek Historical Society.)

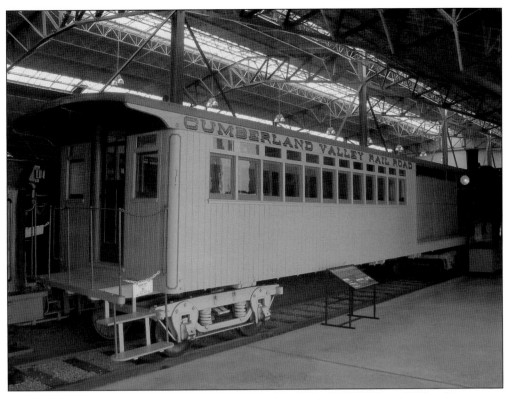

This combination passenger/baggage car was constructed for the CVRR in 1855 and represents the railroad rolling stock that would have been seen on Walnut Street in the 1850s and 1860s. It was donated by the Pennsylvania Railroad to the Railroad Museum of Pennsylvania in Strasburg, where it is displayed. (Author's collection.)

Hagerstown's second town hall was constructed on the southeast corner of Potomac and Franklin Streets in 1818. Prior to this, the town hall was in the middle of Public Square. The tower was heavily altered in the late 1800s, and the building was removed in 1937 to make way for the new city hall, which has been located on this site since it opened in 1941. (City of Hagerstown.)

Kee Mar College opened in 1853 as a collegiate-level institution for young women. Located on a prominent hill on the east side of town, its site was where King Street is today. Kee Mar operated into the 20th century. The Washington County Hospital moved into the former school on April 1, 1912, and remained there for over 98 years until it moved east of the city in late 2010. The building, pictured here around 1857, was used as a Union army headquarters for Gen. Robert Patterson in the summer of 1861 and as a military hospital at various times during the war. The building was removed in the early 20th century. This may be the oldest outdoor photograph of Hagerstown known to exist. (WCHS.)

The John Stull Mill site bears little resemblance to its current appearance. The large frame mill stood on the west bank of the Antietam Creek at the Mount Aetna Road crossing from the 1730s until it burned in 1885. A new mill was then built that survived until 1925. The *c.* 1844 stone arched bridge carried Mount Aetna Road across the famous creek. The site was later bought by the city, and the Municipal Electric Light Plant was constructed to the left. The bridge stood until around 1980 when it had to be replaced with a modern span capable of accommodating the large number of automobiles that travel through that area. A Civil War–era newspaper drawing showing Union troops crossing this bridge on July 12, 1863, can be seen in chapter three. This photograph appears in a stereograph created by Elias Recher around 1880. (WMR-WCFL.)

Another view of the mill, seen from the north. The mill machinery was powered by a waterwheel in Marsh Run. The stream bed was later relocated to run along Memorial Boulevard and enter the Antietam Creek at the Municipal Electric Light Plant. This image also was the artistry of Elias Recher. (WMR-WCFL)

Heyser's Woods was a popular and scenic location on the south edge of town along the Williamsport Road. John H. Heyser (right) constructed his home (below) between 1843 and 1846. Starting in 1854, he allowed the Hagerstown Fair Association to hold fairs here, which were suspended due to the Civil War. Heyser's Woods served as an army campsite at times throughout the war. (WCHS.)

In 1915, the city purchased Heyser's Woods and created City Park. Heyser's home stands today and is known as the City Park Mansion House. Pictured here are John C. Snavely and wife, around 1920. John Snavely was employed by the City of Hagerstown as the park's caretaker. (WMR-WCFL.)

A fugitive from justice in Kansas, abolitionist John Brown checked into the Washington House Hotel on June 30, 1859, using the alias "Isaac Smith." His mission: find a base of operations from which he would launch a slave revolt, targeting the weapons at the U.S. Armory in Harpers Ferry. He quickly leased a property from the estate of Robert Kennedy, located south of Sharpsburg, and began assembling his force and supplies. (WCHS.)

Brown escaped detection by local residents through the use of an alias and changing his appearance. As he was a nationally known fugitive, Hagerstonians would have recognized Brown from newspaper drawings made of this and similar photographs showing him clean-shaven. However, by the time he came to Hagerstown, Brown had grown a full, flowing white beard. The use of the assumed name and beard afforded him the anonymity he needed to execute his plans. (Author's collection.)

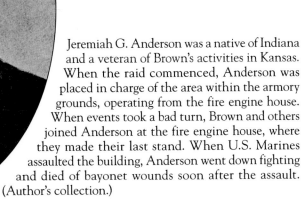

Jeremiah G. Anderson was a native of Indiana and a veteran of Brown's activities in Kansas. When the raid commenced, Anderson was placed in charge of the area within the armory grounds, operating from the fire engine house. When events took a bad turn, Brown and others joined Anderson at the fire engine house, where they made their last stand. When U.S. Marines assaulted the building, Anderson went down fighting and died of bayonet wounds soon after the assault. (Author's collection.)

Owen Brown was his father's chief lieutenant and his hotel roommate at the Washington House. During the raid, he was in charge of a rear guard that remained in Maryland and was also tasked with transporting captured weapons to an abandoned schoolhouse near the Kennedy farm. When he determined that the raid had been foiled and their compatriots were trapped, Owen led his party over the mountains and escaped into Pennsylvania. After the Civil War, he moved to California, where he enjoyed a quiet notoriety as the last survivor of Brown's raiders, passing away in 1891. (Author's collection.)

Oliver Brown was the youngest of Brown's sons to survive to adulthood. When the Kennedy farm was secured, his sister and his wife came to take care of Brown's "army." They were sent home just before the raid. Oliver was one of the few raiders at the engine house who showed a flag of truce, hoping to end the hostilities. But the enraged citizens fired. Mortally wounded, Oliver was dragged back into the engine house. As he was suffering greatly, his irritated father exhorted him to "die like a man." He passed away later that night before the Marine assault began. (Author's collection.)

WASHINGTON HOUSE.

H. YINGLING, PROPRIETOR.

DATE.	1859	TIME.		ROOM.	RESIDENCE.

Last of the John Brown Party — PASADENA, Cal., Jan. 11.—The funeral of Owen Brown, son of John Brown of Ossawatomie, and last survivor of the Harper's Ferry affair, occurred here yesterday. The dead man had for a number of years passed the life of a hermit on a remote summit of the Sierra Madre mountains, known as Brown's Peak. He was 74 years old at the time of his death.

Thursday Cont'd — J Smith & Sons — 6 — New York
Do #A — J G Anderson — 10 — new york
" Do #M — H Dr Minnick —
" #D — Dr W Chaney — West. Co
" Do # — John L McAtee — Princeton College
" Do #1 — W A McAtee — do
" Do #S — Owen Smith — 6 — New York
" Do #S — Oliver Smith — 10 — do
" Do Old — Hand Brumbaugh — Washington Co

The original guest register of the Washington House shows Brown and his son Owen occupied Room 6, and son Oliver and Jeremiah G. Anderson were in Room 10. The Washington House was located on West Washington Street where the University System of Maryland Center at Hagerstown campus is located today. The hotel burned in 1874. (WMR-WCFL.)

A common form of construction in the early days of Hagerstown was the use of local limestone. This building stood on the southwest corner of East Washington Street and Locust Street until replaced by the current Foltz Manufacturing Company building. (*Maryland Cracker Barrel.*)

John Cook was an East Washington Street merchant. After one term as Fifth Ward councilman and five years as city election judge, he was elected mayor. Cook served two 2-year terms as mayor, from 1860 to 1862 and again from 1864 to 1866. He was not involved in any official interaction with Confederate commanders when Hagerstown was ransomed in July 1864. Many elected officials in the region fled north when the Confederates approached in the mistaken fear that they would be made hostages. Lower ranking city officials dealt with the Confederate demands. (City of Hagerstown.)

Mayor Cook fathered a large family. Taken about 1869 by local photographer Elias Recher, this carte de visite shows his daughter Cora Bell Cook, age 10, and son Frank Ephraim Cook, age 4. A family member wrote on the back "awful photo." (Cynthia Blackstock.)

Hagerstown had three fire companies during the Civil War. First Hose Company's 1853 apparatus is shown in the streets of Charles Town, West Virginia, where it was sold to Citizen's Fire Company. Barely visible is "First Hose Co." on the pump tower. (Bill Theriault.)

Lutheran Church.

Before and during the war, the First Hose Company occupied the ornate shed at the front of St. John's Lutheran Church. In the 1880s, they moved to a new facility one block north on South Potomac Street. (City of Hagerstown.)

Antietam Fire Company (Company 2) was housed in a building located on South Jonathan Street (Summit Avenue) directly behind the circuit courthouse. It appears at the right in this drawing. The courthouse was used as an army hospital in 1862 and 1863. Burned in 1871, the courthouse was replaced with the current building soon thereafter. (City of Hagerstown.)

The Independent Junior Fire Company (Company 3), a spin-off of the First Hose Company, constructed a firehouse on the west side of North Potomac Street in 1852. The building was used for various military purposes during the war. Structurally unsound, the building was demolished and a new edifice built in its place in the 1880s that survives to this day. The "Juniors" moved from this site to a new station on Eastern Boulevard in 1992. (City of Hagerstown.)

George Bell was the son of the editor of the *Hagerstown Torchlight* newspaper. He was appointed to the U.S. Military Academy at West Point by congressman James Dixon Roman and graduated in 1853. Bell distinguished himself in 1861 as a courier of secret dispatches for Gen. Winfield Scott. Transferred to the commissary department, he progressed through increasingly responsible posts until he was overseeing the purchase and distribution of food for tens of thousands of troops every day. Bell received a brevet (honorary) promotion to brigadier general in 1865 and retired with the rank of colonel in 1892. His younger brother Henry C. Bell served in the Confederate army as a trooper in Company C, 1st Maryland Cavalry. (USAMHI.)

The Straub home was located on the south side of Washington Avenue and on the west side of Washington Square. The residence was a local landmark during the Civil War era. Soon thereafter, the site was purchased, the house razed, and the first building of St. Mark's Lutheran Church was constructed. The current structure in the western quadrant of Washington Square is the second church building on the site. (WCHS.)

As a young man, Elias Recher became fascinated with the photographic process developed by Louis Daguerre in the 1830s. As early as 1855, Recher established a studio near Public Square, which flourished for many years. He later expanded his portrait business to include mass-produced stereographs of regional scenery, most notably the Antietam battlefield and Pen Mar Park. Many of the portraits and postwar stereographs included throughout this book are his work. (WCHS.)

Two

OFF TO WAR AND SOLDIERS COME TO HAGERSTOWN
1860–1862

Among the first soldiers to enter Hagerstown was a company of Pennsylvania Militia commanded by Capt. William McMullen. Known as "McMullen's Rangers," they mustered into service on May 20, 1861, and served 90 days. Formed mostly from firemen of the Moyamensing Hose Company in South Philadelphia, the group was part of Gen. Robert Patterson's force. This image of McMullen's Rangers at Patterson's Kee Mar College headquarters appeared in the nationally circulated *Harper's Weekly* magazine on July 20, 1861. Hagerstown is seen in the background, with the tall spire of St. John's Lutheran Church near center. Captain McMullen later went on to notoriety in Philadelphia as a boss in the political establishment of the City of Brotherly Love. (Tim Snyder.)

MAJOR-GENERAL PATTERSON.—From a Photograph.

Robert Patterson was an aging veteran of the War of 1812. When war erupted, he was assigned by Washington to secure the Hagerstown-Cumberland-Martinsburg area. Patterson made his headquarters at Kee Mar College. In July, Confederates at Harpers Ferry slipped away unnoticed and reinforced other Confederates near Manassas, which contributed to the first battle of the war being a Confederate victory. Looking to lay blame for the fiasco, the War Department focused on several officers including Patterson. After Congressional hearings, he was relieved of further duty. (Tim Snyder.)

Dewitt Clinton Rench (pictured here in his Baltimore Militia uniform) was raised just south of Hagerstown. A vocal reb, Rench was in a store in Williamsport when a pro-Union mob gathered. They demanded he leave town, and a fight ensued in which Rench was killed. When word spread to his friends in the Confederate force encamped across the Potomac River, the officers had difficultly controlling their men, who wanted to burn the town in retaliation. Initially buried on his family farm, he was removed to Rose Hill Cemetery in Hagerstown after the war. (Courtesy of Dave Mark.)

In September 1861, soldiers arrived at the home of Dr. Charles MacGill to arrest him for his vocal support of the South. A misunderstanding led to a scuffle in which his son was injured and his daughter came to her father's and brother's defense, thrashing the soldiers with a buggy whip. Dr. MacGill was transported to Fort McHenry, then to Fort Warren in Boston. Refusing to sign a loyalty oath, he was released unconditionally a year later. MacGill had four sons who served the Confederacy, and he would join them in 1863. The home, no longer standing, was located at the current site of 43 South Potomac Street. (WCHS.)

St. John's Episcopal Church started as a small chapel. In 1785, a new church was constructed on a site on South Mulberry Street now only containing the congregation's cemetery. This building was St. John's third home. Opened in 1832, it was located on South Jonathan Street (Summit Avenue) between the courthouse and Antietam Street. In 1871, a nearby building fire cascaded embers onto the church, which also erupted in flames. The congregation then built its current home on South Prospect Street, which was completed in 1873. (WMR-WCFL.)

Marching off to war in 1861 was more social event and less struggle. Much of the baggage that accompanied the troops would be dispensed with as the war progressed. In June 1861, the 1st Wisconsin Volunteer Infantry Regiment arrived in Hagerstown and pitched camp. Some of the soldiers, former newspapermen, created a regimental newspaper that espoused of what was going on in the regiment. A 90-days regiment, the 1st Wisconsin mustered out on August 22. (WMR-WCFL.)

CAMP RECORD.

PRINTED AND PUBLISHED BY THE FIRST REGIMENT OF WISCONSIN VOLUNTEERS.

"HEAD OF COLUMN, FORWARD"—Napoleon.

VOL. 1.   CAMP NEGLEY, HAGERSTOWN, MARYLAND, THURSDAY, JUNE 27TH, 1861.   NO. 1.

Heyser's Silver Cornet Band was a regular presence at gatherings in the 1850s. George Heyser (right), brother of John who appeared in chapter one, was the bandleader. At the end of the war, the band reorganized, perhaps to take advantage of the new flood of musicians being discharged from the army who had learned their art in the service. (WCHS.)

Edward Mobley was the sheriff in 1861. He lived with his large family in the jailer's house on North Jonathan Street. In response to a call for volunteers for the Union, Mobley recruited a company that mustered in August 1862 as Company A, 7th Maryland Infantry. Somewhere during this time, Mobley moved his family from the jailer's house to a home on East Washington Street so that they could be nearer his parents during his absence. Mobley was wounded twice in 1864, including a serious injury to the neck. By the time the regiment mustered out, Mobley was a major, and he commanded the regiment in some of the hottest action in the waning days of the war. Active in civic affairs and the Grand Army of the Republic (GAR), he lived on North Locust Street in his golden years. (Charles Mobley.)

This photograph, taken years after the war, depicts the interior yard of the Washington County Jail, where Sheriff Mobley presided over activities. Although capital punishment was rare, it was administered locally until the early 20th century, when the state assumed control of all executions. One hanging was held during the war, in 1863. The people standing on the gallows are unidentified. (*Maryland Cracker Barrel.*)

This 1887 drawing shows the Washington County Jail as it appeared during the Civil War. The jail sat to the rear, adjacent to West Church Street, while the jailer's office and residence faced Jonathan Street. The lockup housed criminals as well as captured runaway slaves being held until their owners could claim them. A chain of men occupied the office of sheriff during the war—including Mobley (1859–1861), Henry Gantz (1861–1863), Samuel Oliver (1863–1865) and Jonathan Newcomer (1865–1867). (WCHS.)

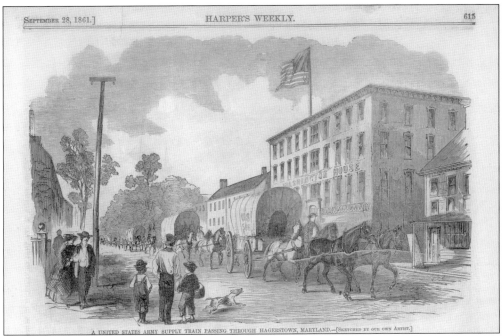

A UNITED STATES ARMY SUPPLY TRAIN PASSING THROUGH HAGERSTOWN, MARYLAND.—[SKETCHED BY OUR OWN ARTIST.]

Hagerstown once again appeared in national press on September 21, 1861, when *Harper's Weekly* printed this drawing of a U.S. Army supply train heading eastbound on Washington Street in front of the Washington House hotel. The pro-Northern sentiments of the hotel owner are exhibited by the large national colors flying from the roof. (Tim Snyder.)

This 1906 image of a covered wagon made by local photographer Bascom Phreaner illustrates the type of vehicle settlers used as they drove through Hagerstown via the National Road on their way west. (Author's collection.)

During the winter of 1861–1862, the 13th Massachusetts Infantry Regiment was the garrison force that patrolled the upper Potomac River area. Its main camp, Camp Jackson, was located east of Williamsport on the north side of the Boonsboro Road (the location of today's Williamsport High School and the Interstate Industrial Park). These men served as Hagerstown's provost marshal (military police). This photograph shows the cookhouse where Company K prepared its meals. (Brad Forbush.)

While surgeon Allston W. Whitney and assistant surgeon John Theodore Heard lived in tents, a building was constructed for the care of their patients. Here men are pictured standing in front of the 13th Massachusetts Regiment Hospital at Camp Jackson. (Brad Forbush.)

Lt. Charles B. Fox of Company K, 13th Massachusetts relaxes in his tent outside of Hagerstown. The men outside are wearing peculiar headgear. Later Captain Fox was commissioned lieutenant colonel of the 55th Massachusetts Infantry Regiment, an African-American regiment. (USAMHI– Massachusetts Commandery, MOLLUS Collection.)

Even when on campaign, much baggage accompanied a 1,000-man regiment. Here the supply wagons of the 13th Massachusetts Infantry are shown in their "wagon park" outside of camp. (USAMHI–Massachusetts Commandery, MOLLUS Collection.)

On December 15, 1861, 13th Massachusetts bandsman Edwin Rice (believed to be the bearded man at the left of the third row) wrote home: "Wednesday, the band went to Hagerstown to have a photograph taken. The artist could not take a photograph outdoors, so we cuddled up into a heap in his room and he took us the best he could, which is not saying a great deal for him." The photographer was Elias Recher. (Historical Image Bank.)

Local African Americans found good employment in tending to the needs of soldiers who traveled in and out of the area. Here, a group of "contrabands" poses for a photograph in the 13th Massachusetts Infantry Regiment's camp near Hagerstown. The second lady from the right holds a lovely bonnet. (USAMHI–Massachusetts Commandery, MOLLUS Collection.)

Soldiers would find ways to socialize with the local populace in the areas where they were stationed. After some locals heard the 13th Massachusetts Regiment's glee club in camp, they convinced the soldiers to perform for the citizens of Hagerstown. Posters such as this one advertised the show, which was held on January 15, 1862, at the lyceum. Band member Edwin Rice attended the performance. He gave it moderate reviews in a letter home. (American Antiquarian Society.)

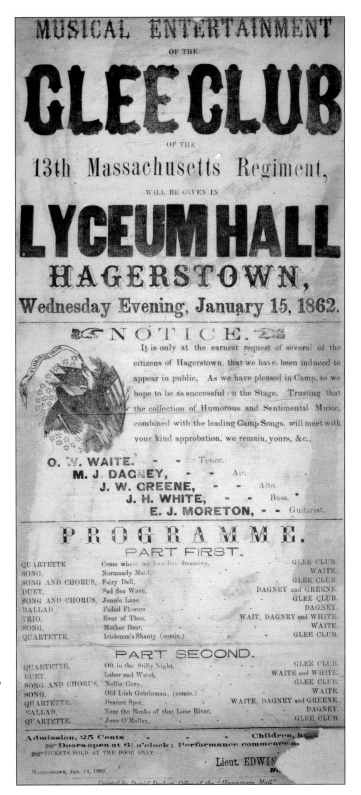

Photographed in Hagerstown, the 13th Massachusetts Glee Club consists of, from left to right, (first row) club manager Lt. Edwin Frost and Sgt. Walter H. Wentworth; (second row) Hospital Steward John H. White, Pvt. John Green, Cpl. Michael Dagney, and Pvt. Osgood W. Waitt. (Brad Forbush.)

The Hagerstown Lyceum was a performance and meeting hall located on West Washington Street, two doors east of the courthouse. Built in 1844, it had two storefronts on the ground level to provide rents to support the operation, while the public hall was located on the second floor. Little is known of this building. In a letter home, bandsman Edwin Rice wrote that "there was a very fine fresco painting in the hall." (City of Hagerstown.)

Born in Wales, John Rowlands immigrated to Louisiana and adopted the name Henry Morton Stanley. He later joined the Confederate army and was captured and "galvanized" (joined the Union army to avoid prison camp). Discharged in the summer of 1862 at Harpers Ferry due to illness, he headed north on foot. He got as far as Tilghmanton when his sickness forced him to stop. A local farmer allowed him to stay in his barn for a few weeks then took him to Hagerstown and purchased him a train ticket north. Stanley went on to fame as a journalist. His reporting led to his search in Africa for a missing missionary. Upon finding the subject of his search, Stanley reportedly uttered the famous question, "Dr. Livingstone, I presume?" (Author's collection.)

Susan South Freaner was the daughter of a Hagerstown policeman. Her brother George served on the staff of Confederate general J. E. B. Stuart. Freaner was educated at a Catholic girls school in Ohio. During the war, she worked as a nurse in the army hospitals in Hagerstown. Later, Freaner returned to Ohio and converted to Catholicism, entering the Order of St. Ursula. She helped found a girls' high school in Cincinnati which functions to this day. Elevated through the ranks of her order, she took the name Mother Baptista. She was described by Pres. Theodore Roosevelt as "one woman in a million." (Freaner descendants.)

During the Antietam Campaign, the crew of a Franklin Railroad train made its usual run into Hagerstown only to find that when it entered "Angle's Cut," it was in the middle of a Confederate army camp. The crew immediately reversed gears and fled north toward Pennsylvania. Angle's Cut is located on the west side of North Burhans Boulevard, where it crosses the railroad tracks and the quarry at Mitchell Avenue. (*Maryland Cracker Barrel.*)

Knodle's Band was a local civilian brass band that performed throughout Washington County. According to a note that accompanied the image, this daguerreotype was made in the 1850s on the porch of the "old home" in Fairplay. (Greg French.)

NOTICE
TO
MARYLANDERS

☞ **Notice is hereby given that Major**
ROBERT SWAN, of Md., late of the 1st Virginia Cavalry, is authorized by the Secretary of War, to raise a Battalion of Cavalry of Marylanders, under the following grant:

Confederate States of America,
WAR DEPARTMENT, *Adjt. & Ins. Genl's Office,*
Richmond, Va., May 20, 1863.

Authority is hereby granted to Major Robert Swan to raise a Battalion of Cavalry of Marylanders, for the Provisional Army, which may be enlarged to a Regiment formed of men of similar nativity.
Company officers Will be elected, and the several companies composing the organization will be mustered into the service of the Confederate States for the War, and copies of the Muster Rolls, and Election Returns forwarded for file in this office.
By command of the Secretary of War,
SAMUEL W. MILLER, Maj. & A. A. G.

Such as may be disposed to enrol themselves under this authority will call upon the undersigned, at Hagerstown. Now is the time to strike to relieve the State from the grasp of an abolition despotism.

THE VICTORIOUS CONFEDERATE ARMY

has crossed the Potomac, and is now striking as well for the deliverance of Maryland as to secure the independence and liberty of the whole South. Those who may wish to share in the glory of the achievement should lose no time in repairing to the field.
ROBERT SWAN.

Hagerstown, June 27, 1863.

The South's first invasion of the North in 1862 was motivated by the need for a victory on Union soil (which would help the Confederate cause with foreign governments), the need to relieve northern Virginia of the ravages of the war, and to lure Maryland into the Confederacy. Each time the Confederates entered Maryland, there was a concerted effort to recruit Marylanders into service, but this mostly pro-Union area provided only a trickle of recruits. One rebel groused that, if Washington County was any indication of statewide sentiment, Maryland would never be lured away from the Union. This poster displayed in town during the Gettysburg Campaign in 1863 is indicative of the notices that were posted during Lee's first invasion a year earlier in 1862. Maj. Robert Swan, a native of Cumberland, was married to a Hagerstown lady, one of Dr. Charles MacGill's daughters. (Joe Bloom.)

Theodore R. Davis worked as a war correspondent and artist for *Harper's Weekly*. He would send reports and drawings to the magazine for publication. Staff engravers would turn Davis' drawings into wood engravings to appear in the magazine. The image below and several of the illustrations in this book are based on his sketches. Davis was one of the most prolific war artists of the Civil War. His work was published throughout the war, and many of his drawings are among the most recognizable of the period. (USAMHI–Massachusetts Commandery, MOLLUS Collection.)

Confederates under Gen. James Longstreet occupied Hagerstown before the Battle of Antietam. This image from *Harper's Weekly*, published on September 27, 1862, shows Confederates on the grounds of Kee Mar College (today's King Street) looking west, with the spires and cupolas of the town in the distance. This engraving was made from sketches provided by war artist Theodore Davis. (Tim Snyder.)

Davis's drawings focusing on Hagerstown once again appeared in *Harper's Weekly* on October 11, 1862. Here he depicts Kenly's Brigade (Union) marching out of town on September 19th to join McClellan's army. The brigade was recently mustered and hastily trained "fresh fish." It included Hagerstown's own Company A, under Captain Mobley. The author believes that Davis was standing on the west side of Walnut Street behind St. Mary's Church and facing east to sketch this image, the cupola being one on a Methodist church one block east on Jonathan Street. (Tim Snyder.)

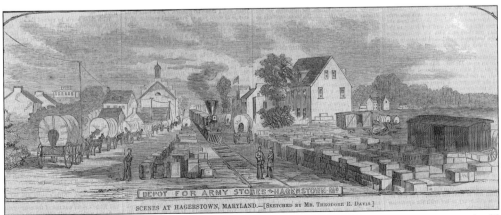

SCENES AT HAGERSTOWN, MARYLAND.—[Sketched by Mr. Theodore R. Davis.]

A *Harper's Weekly* caption on October 18, 1862, reads, "The depot at Hagerstown is a scene of wild activity. Immense stores of all kinds are pouring in for the subsistence of the army; every available foot of space is covered with barrels, bales and boxes." The area Davis shows here is located on Walnut Street looking south toward Washington Street. The back of St. Mary's Catholic Church is to the left of the railroad engine. (Tim Snyder.)

With Davis' fascination with Hagerstown apparently on the wane, the last two images appeared in the October 18, 1862, issue of *Harper's*. Here Davis depicts the Confederates "helping themselves to the flour in Andrew Hager's mills." Hager advised them to eat it, or it might not benefit them much. The event proved his wisdom, "for our cavalry recaptured a part of the wagon train containing this identical flour." Hagers Mill still stands on Mill Street, and the miller's house on the right also exists today. The house is owned by the city and is now the centerpiece of Hager Park. (Tim Snyder.)

Virginian John Gaines was the first doctor on the scene of the famous murder of Col. Elmer Ellsworth in Alexandria on May 24, 1861. As surgeon of the 8th Virginia Infantry, he was captured at Boonsboro when left behind to tend the wounded at South Mountain. Exchanged, Gaines was captured again at Williamsport in 1863 and briefly assigned to the prisoner hospital in Hagerstown. He settled in Boonsboro after the war. Gaines retired to Hagerstown in the 1890s, building a home at 465 North Potomac Street that still stands. (Doug Bast, Boonsboro Museum of History)

Thousands of wounded soldiers, from both North and South, were brought to Hagerstown for care and transport to more distant hospitals. Hagerstown was also the nearest rail depot to send supplies in support of the army. Frances Kennedy opened her home on West Washington Street to wounded Union officers. Known as the Rochester House, it stood until the 1950s. (Library of Congress.)

A young Capt. Oliver Wendell Holmes Jr., of the 20th Massachusetts Infantry, was wounded in the neck at Antietam and brought to Hagerstown. When his father (a famous poet at the time) learned of his son's condition, he traveled from Boston to find his son and arrange for his care. In the chaotic aftermath of the battle, the elder Holmes's search was fruitless, but he kept a journal of his trip that was published in the *Atlantic Magazine* under the title "My Hunt for the Captain." It became one of the father's most recognized writings. Young Oliver later became an associate justice of the U.S. Supreme Court. (USAMHI–Massachusetts Commandery, MOLLUS Collection.)

Surgeon Charles Marcellus Chandler of the 6th Connecticut Infantry Regiment was one of the medical officers detailed to care for wounded troops in Hagerstown. Chandler commanded the Courthouse and Lyceum Hospitals on West Washington Street. (USAMHI–Massachusetts Commandery, MOLLUS Collection.)

Regardless of the privations war brought, the citizens of Hagerstown were widely praised in the national press for their care of the wounded after Antietam. Here Theodore Davis again provides national coverage to Hagerstown in the October 11, 1862, copy of *Harper's Weekly*. In his reports, Davis heaped much praise on the citizens of Hagerstown, saying the people were bringing supplies and fresh-cooked food at all hours of the day and night to the hospitals that dotted the city. (Tim Snyder.)

One curiosity of which Hagerstown could boast was its own telescope and observatory. George R. Bowman was an avid astronomer, and he dispersed tokens like the one shown here, allowing visitors to gaze at the stars. It is not clear if this was a side business with an admission fee or if he used it as a marketing tool to generate traffic to his bakery. (Stacks Rare Coins.)

Local native George R. Bowman was a confectioner and baker. He took on apprentices, including William Seidenstricker, who later served as a captain in the 13th Maryland Infantry. Bowman's business prospered from the 1850s until his retirement in the 1880s. A photograph of his West Washington Street business and a unique story associated with his wife, Catharine, and her sister Margaret Greenawalt can be found in chapter three. (WCHS.)

James Ireland served in Company A, 29th Pennsylvania Infantry Regiment. The Pennsylvanians were stationed in Hagerstown in the fall of 1862. An amateur artist, he crafted at least two paintings of buildings in town. His depiction above shows the company in front of the Independent Junior Hose Company on North Potomac Street. Close examination reveals a painstaking attention to detail, showing the pumper in the open bay, a sign over the door, and a soldier Ireland identifies as himself in front of the building. A painting of the courthouse also survives. (Doug Bast, Boonsboro Museum of History.)

This house was located to the north of the Stull Mill along Antietam Creek. The intersection of Eastern Boulevard and Cannon Avenue marks its approximate location. (This residence is visible in the background of the photograph of the mill found on page 20.) With a commanding view of the Mount Aetna bridge over the Antietam Creek and not far from Andrew Hager's Mill on the National Road, the home's occupants surely witnessed the comings and goings of many thousands of soldiers. Purchased after the Civil War by the Rowland family, it was their home for many years. The Rowlands operated the old Stull mill in the late 19th century. This image was taken from a c. 1880 stereograph captured by Elias Recher. (WMR-WCFL.)

THE TOWN HALL, HAGERSTOWN, MD, GUARDED BY THE DAHLGREN HOWITZER BATTERY, OF PHILADELPHIA. SKETCHED BY OUR SPECIAL ARTIST. See page 355.

In the aftermath of Antietam, militia and other "deep reserve" units were brought to Hagerstown to assist in the recovery efforts. Here a drawing from the *New York Illustrated* magazine shows a Dahlgren naval howitzer from Philadelphia that was acquired as part of the security detail and was so placed in front of the town hall, where it could sweep Potomac Street. Naval howitzers were not commonly used by the army. Therefore its appearance in Hagerstown would have been unusual. The large presence of Union forces in Hagerstown did not prevent J. E. B. Stuart's cavalry from raiding Franklin County, Pennsylvania, in early October. (Ted Alexander.)

This ambrotype was found in the grave of a Union soldier at Antietam at the end of the war and brought to Hagerstown, where Bascom Phreaner photographed it as a reproducible carte de visite. Historians have concluded that this was done to circulate it in northern newspapers, hoping someone would recognize the young woman and be able to identify the soldier who carried it. A similar event occurred at Gettysburg when a photograph of three children was found on the body of a Union infantry sergeant. Circulation of the image in the press resulted in the children being recognized as the family of Sgt. Amos Humiston, allowing him to be identified. Historians, however, have been unable to find evidence that copies of this photograph were circulated. It appears the man was never identified. (New York Public Library via Dr. Thomas Clemens.)

Copied from an Ambrotype found in the grave of an Unknown Soldier on the Battle Field of Antietam.

PHOTOGRAPHED
BY
B. W. T. PHREANER
Hagerstown, Md.

No. ....

Copies of this picture can be had at any time.

Three

WAR IN THE STREETS
1863

Prior to the Civil War, a group of local slaves formed a brass band and performed in what is now Jacob Wheaton Park. It was known as the Robert Moxley Band, named after the bandmaster. In 1863, the army began recruiting African Americans into segregated units. A recruiting officer saw the band perform and was so impressed that he arranged for the entire band to be enlisted as a unit. Designated the Number One Brigade Band, United States Colored Troops, it performed at recruiting drives promoting African American enlistment. It also served in the Petersburg Campaign before being transferred to Texas where the band mustered out in 1866. No photographs of the unit survive, but it would have appeared very much like the regimental band of the 107th United States Colored Infantry, pictured here. (Library of Congress.)

Young Leighton Parks lived with his mother on South Prospect Street. Robert E. Lee knew his father in the army. In June 1863, Lee invited the family to visit his headquarters near today's Hickory Elementary School. Armed with a pail of raspberries, Leighton was the only Parks who visited. He offered a diversion for the homesick generals. Lee walked him on his horse, Traveller. General Longstreet, still recovering from the loss of his three youngest children the year before in a scarlet fever epidemic, enjoyed time bouncing Leighton on his knee. (WMR-WCFL.)

Ebenezer African Methodist Episcopal Church stood on Bethel Street from 1840 until it was rebuilt in 1910. In January 1863, several African Americans in town contracted smallpox. Fearing an epidemic, the town leased the basement for three months as a hospital "with arrangements for furnishing food and making them as comfortable as possible." Dr. W. H. Lee cared for the sick, and local African Americans Thomas Henry and Jacob Wheaton were hired as steward and nurse. It is believed the church may have been used as a military hospital at times during the war. (Marguerite Doleman Collection.)

The annual election for city council was held around April 1, 1863. During the war, many communities settled on a "Union Ticket" and avoided contested elections that might serve to further divide the populace. This ballot from the 1863 election was recently discovered in the city council's mid-19th century minutes book. Citizens would vote by handing a copy of the ballot to the election judge. The judge would then deposit the ballots into a box to be counted when the polls closed. (City of Hagerstown.)

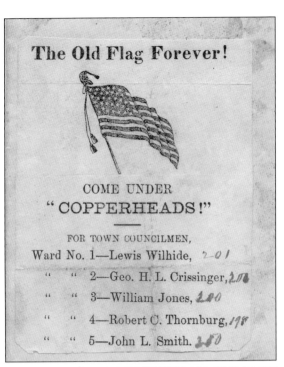

The Old Flag Forever!

COME UNDER
" COPPERHEADS !"

FOR TOWN COUNCILMEN,

Ward No. 1—Lewis Wilhide, 2 0 1
"   "   2—Geo. H. L. Crissinger, 2,04
"   "   3—William Jones, 2 0 0
"   "   4—Robert C. Thornburg, 198
"   "   5—John L. Smith. 2 0 0

After passing through Hagerstown in late June, the Army of Northern Virginia met disaster at Gettysburg on July 3. Torrential rains pounded the exhausted armies on July 4 and 5 as the rebels struggled to put an army and its thousands of supply wagons and ambulances full of thousands of wounded into motion. The rains quickly drove the Potomac River to flood stage, meaning the Union army could potentially trap the crippled Confederate forces before they could reach the relative safety of Virginia. (Author's collection.)

Regardless of the miserable weather, the Union army moved to harass the retreating Confederates. General Meade's infantry mostly marched toward Frederick to keep between the rebels and Washington, then turned west toward Williamsport hoping to cut off the Confederate withdrawal. Union cavalry attacked the Confederate trains at Monterrey and west of Cashtown, Pennsylvania. The warring armies crawled slowly through the mud toward Hagerstown. At 3:00 a.m. on July 5, troopers of the 1st Vermont Cavalry attacked a Confederate train at Leitersburg and captured 100 men and their wagons. So fatigued were the men of both sides that one reported "never had the men and horses been so jaded and stove up. One of our men who dropped at the foot of a tree in a sort of a hollow, went to sleep, and continued sleeping until the water rose to his waist . . . battery horses would drop in their traces . . . the men and officers on horseback would go to sleep without knowing it." Other battles occurred in the area between July 5 and July 11, including such places as Cearfoss, Clear Spring, Smithsburg, and Boonsboro. This *c.* 1900 photograph of Leitersburg gives the reader an accurate view of what the weary cavalrymen and teamsters would have seen in town 37 years earlier. Pictured are Abraham Lincoln Smith; his wife, Catherine; and their daughters Maude and Sarah in front of the family's tavern on the town square. (Dorothy Smith.)

On July 6, 1863, combat reached the doorsteps of every Hagerstonian. Learning of a Confederate wagon train vulnerable to capture, Gen. Hugh Judson Kilpatrick (right) moved north from Boonsboro and ordered a charge into Hagerstown in an attempt to snare vital supplies. The battle opened around St. John's Lutheran Church, where barricades were manned by the depleted ranks of the 9th and 10th Virginia Cavalry Regiments. They were overrun by squadrons from the 18th Pennsylvania, 1st Vermont, and 1st West Virginia Cavalry Regiments. The Yanks charged north from the area of today's Rose Hill Cemetery. (Library of Congress.)

In addition to the Virginians posted on the south end of town, a small brigade of North Carolina cavalry under Brig. Gen. Beverly Robertson (left) took up a defensive position on the northern edge of the city. With fewer than a thousand men and horses, Robertson's role was to keep the Union cavalry away from the wagon train and buy time until a stronger body of infantry could be brought into the fight. (Library of Congress.)

The rain-soaked and exhausted troopers of Chambliss's and Robertson's Brigades (the vanguard of the Army of Northern Virginia and guardians of the wagon train) entered Hagerstown from the north (rear center). Robertson took up position north of Public Square and Chambliss's men built barricades just south of St. John's Lutheran Church. This photograph was taken from the steeple of St. John's just after the war. The barriers would have been behind the photographer. Arriving from Boonsboro, General Kilpatrick ordered an assault on the barricades. His men stormed north up South Potomac Street and breached the makeshift walls. The rebels were overwhelmed and retreated north and regrouped around Public Square. The commander at the barricades, Col. J. Lucius Davis of the 10th Virginia Cavalry was captured when his wounded horse fell and pinned him to the street. Yet he continued to fight while pinned beneath the horse. Nicknamed "Killcavalry" by his men, General Kilpatrick ordered his forces to pursue the rebels north on Potomac Street (in the center of this image), and a great cavalry clash occurred in and around Public Square. (WCHS.)

This 18th-century dwelling stood on the west side of South Potomac Street across from today's Washington County Free Library's central facility. It was demolished around 1912 to make way for an Odd Fellows Lodge that stands to this day. Countless soldiers marched past this house during the war; and in the battle on July 6, the cavalrymen of the 9th and 10th Virginia Regiments swept past its door with Col. Nathaniel Richmond's Union troopers in hot pursuit. (*Maryland Cracker Barrel*.)

During the Civil War, Justus Heiml operated a store and brewery on his property on the west side of South Potomac Street. This site is located to the right of the Maryland Theater and is now occupied by a four-story apartment building. In this late 1800s photograph, Heiml's brewery looks much as it would have to the blue and gray soldiers who fought their way up Potomac Street. (WCHS.)

The building that later housed Ordway's Pianos and Organs was located on the east side of Public Square in the late 1800s. The first two floors of this structure stood during the battle in the square; the third floor was added later. This site is now occupied by the Alexander House. (*Maryland Cracker Barrel.*)

The troopers of the 9th and 10th Virginia Regiments fled north from the church in the background. When their pursuers reached the square, 40 men from the 1st Maryland Cavalry crashed into the blue cavalry from West Washington Street (to the right). This checked the pursuit and afforded the Virginians time to regroup two blocks to the north. Andrew Hager operated a store on the site of Roessner's Confectionery in 1863. (WCHS.)

Capt. Frank A. Bond commanded the small band of Marylanders. Born in Harford County, he was a resident of Anne Arundel County. After the war, he became the warden of the Maryland House of Correction in Jessup and received a commission in the Maryland National Guard, rising to the rank of general. Bond was wounded in the leg later on July 6 in the pursuit of Kilpatrick's men toward Williamsport. This wound would preclude further field service. He was serving on the staff of Gen. Collett Leventhorpe at the war's end. (Dr. Mark Bond.)

With the sound of the guns, Col. Milton Ferguson's brigade rode hard from Chewsville to aid their fellow Confederates. Ferguson's force entered the fray from Chewsville Pike (now Jefferson Boulevard) and took positions in the area of today's city golf course. An artillery duel rocked the homes of Hagerstown to their foundations when a battery commanded by Capt. Roger Preston Chew of nearby Charles Town (left) unlimbered his guns and began shelling the arriving Union cavalry. (Author's collection.)

Battery E, 4th U.S. Artillery was ordered to the high ground on the north side of Kee Mar College. Commanded by Lt. Samuel Elder (standing far left), the troops dueled with Chew's battery for about 30 minutes and fired into Ferguson's force with grape and cannister (short range antipersonnel ammunition). Elder's hilltop position was reinforced by elements of the 5th New York and 1st Vermont Cavalry Regiments. This photograph of Elder and his fellow officers was taken about six weeks after the battle. (Library of Congress.)

Kee Mar College occupied the heights at present-day King Street. Its elevation and minimal number of trees made the site optimal for placing artillery, as it commanded a sweeping view of the battlefield. Although the Confederates were on the defensive in town, Ferguson's brigade arriving from Chewsville was on the offensive. However, the commanding location enabled Elder's battery and its cavalry support from the New Yorkers and Vermonters to fend off several attacks and attempts to swing around the right of the Union line. After the Battle of Hagerstown, the college was once again commandeered for military use as a field hospital. (WCHS.)

When Kilpatrick prepared another assault, Capt. Ulric Dahlgren (standing) volunteered to lead it. He dismounted 20 men from the 18th Pennsylvania Cavalry and the small force made its way up Potomac Street toward the square, 10 on each sidewalk and Dahlgren riding in the street. They reached Franklin Street before fire from a church and the Oak Spring to their left (west) checked their advance. Dahlgren was shot in the right ankle. He is shown here about a month before the battle. Kneeling next to him is Prussian count Ferdinand von Zeppelin, who later popularized air travel in dirigibles. (Library of Congress.)

The walls and fences around Oak Spring (now the location of the Pioneer Hook and Ladder Company) and an adjacent church provided Confederates excellent cover from which to fire into the left flank of the attacking Union cavalry. This image is taken from Franklin Street looking south toward Washington Street (WCHS.)

The 20 troopers from the 18th Pennsylvania Cavalry who charged up the sidewalks of North Potomac Street would have encountered this view, minus the wheelmen and throngs of spectators. This early 1880s image from a wheelmen's convention shows a streetscape little changed in 20 years. The Franklin Hotel can be seen at left, as well as the cupolas of the Independent Junior Fire Company (left) and Hagerstown Town Hall (right). To the right of the photograph, a sergeant was struck down in the service of his country when an unidentified Hagerstown woman fired at the troops from an upper window. (WCHS.)

This faded stereograph image from the late 1860s or early 1870s places the viewer in the boots of the Confederate cavalrymen as they watched Kilpatrick's Union horsemen storm up Potomac Street into the city. The gallant Captain Dahlgren was wounded in the area shown in the right foreground of this photograph. The town hall is conspicuous on the left, with the spire of St. John's Lutheran Church visible in the distance. (WCHS.)

The Oak Spring Church was constructed in 1855 on the south side of West Franklin Street between Potomac Street and today's Pioneer Hook and Ladder Company building. It served as a good barrier to shield Confederate marksmen shooting into the Union cavalry advancing up Potomac Street past the town hall. The church congregation relocated farther west on Franklin Street in the late 1800s; it is now Christ Reformed Church. (*Maryland Cracker Barrel.*)

The residence of Dr. James B. McKee near the Independent Junior Fire Company was approximately the farthest point north to which Union cavalry advanced. With flanking fire from the Oak Spring and an opponent taking full advantage of the tall wall at Zion Reformed Church, the Union advance stalled in the face of numbers, superior position, and geography. (WCHS.)

71

As Union soldiers fell, they were hurried by their comrades and local men into nearby buildings such as the Franklin Hotel. The hotel served as a hospital at times throughout the war and was situated where the North Potomac Street parking deck is located today. (Roger Keller.)

WITHIN THIS WALL IS DEPOSITED THE LEG OF COL ULRIC DAHLGREN U S V WOUNDED JULY 6TH 1863 WHILE SKIRMISHING IN THE STREETS OF HAGERSTOWN WITH THE REBELS AFTER THE BATTLE OF GETTYSBURGH

Captain Dahlgren was taken to his father's home in Washington. Gangrene set in, and the foot had to be amputated at the lower leg. An admiral in the U.S. Navy, Dahlgren's father had the leg buried in the wall of a building at the Washington Navy Yard. Captain Dahlgren was promoted to colonel and was killed in a raid on Richmond on March 2, 1864. Controversy ensued when Confederates found orders on his body that called for burning the city and assassinating Pres. Jefferson Davis and his cabinet. His father spent the rest of his life trying to clear Ulric's name. (Maryland Cracker Barrel.)

Zion Reformed Church was constructed in the 1770s. The Confederate defensive line took full advantage of both the church's placement on a hill and the stone retaining wall that runs along West Church Street to create an impenetrable barrier to the attacking Union horsemen. After the Confederates evacuated town a week later, Gen. George Custer observed Confederate movements from the steeple. A sharpshooter's bullet is said to have ricocheted off of the church bell, nearly cutting Custer's career short. (City of Hagerstown.)

The actions of Chambliss and Robertson and the little band of Marylanders bought time for a brigade of North Carolina infantry under Gen. Alfred Iverson (left) to hurry to the front and develop a defensive position at Zion Church. Iverson also sent men forward to occupy houses and buildings in the block between the church and town hall to create sniper's nests. With this development and Col. Ferguson making progress at Kee Mar College, Kilpatrick withdrew his forces and moved to reinforce another Union brigade attacking Williamsport. (Library of Congress.)

This photograph of North Potomac Street in 1867 is believed to be published here for the first time. The streetscape is little changed from the great cavalry battle four years earlier. Captain Dahlgren's 20 troopers ran up the sidewalks seen here toward the Confederates awaiting around Zion Reformed Church. The church was reconstructed to its current appearance in 1867. This image shows scaffolding erected to dismantle its pre–Civil War steeple. The weather vane Little

Heiskell, which appears on page 2, can barely be seen as a ghostly image above the ball at the top of the cupola of the Hagerstown Town Hall. The 1818 town hall was demolished in the 1930s to make way for the current city hall. Captain Dahlgren was wounded in front of this building at the intersection of Potomac and Franklin Streets. (WCHS.)

In the preparation of this book, the following note was discovered on the back of this *c.* 1890 image of Margaret Greenawalt at the Washington County Historical Society: "waived the flag over retreating Confederate soldiers and was roundly cursed as they sped up West Washington Street while her sister, Mrs. Bowman pulled at her skirt and begged her to come in saying 'they'll shoot you Maggie, they'll shoot you!'. Miss Margaret was standing on the iron balcony where the hardware store is now - then bakery - waving the flag to the soldiers in blue just coming through the square below." Is it possible Hagerstown can boast of its own Barbara Fritchie? (WCHS.)

Myra L. McDade (the author of the note on the back of Maggie's photograph) wrote the following on the back of this image of Mrs. Bowman: "told me the story of her sister several times when I was 12 years old." Catharine and George Bowman ran a successful confectionery and bakery business on West Washington Street from the 1850s to the 1880s. Maggie lived with them. The Bowmans retired in the 1880s and purchased a house on Broadway, and Maggie stayed with them. After Catharine passed away in 1906, Maggie moved to Yonkers, New York, to live with Clyde Furst, her grandnephew (Catharine's grandson) until she too passed in 1911. These photographs were taken about 30 years after their encounter with the Confederate army. (WCHS.)

Since the only time Confederates "retreated" through town was after Gettysburg, Maggie's brave act likely occurred during the street battle in July 1863. This 1862 image by Elias Recher shows the George R. Bowman Confectioners and Bakery on the south side of West Washington Street. It is the checkered building at the extreme right. This is the building on which Bowman kept his telescope and observatory (mentioned on page 53). The Updegraff hat store building on the left still stands. (WCHS.)

Col. Samuel Lumpkin of the 44th Georgia Infantry was wounded on the first day of the Battle of Gettysburg. His leg amputated, Lumpkin was loaded into a wagon and endured a horrific, rain-soaked journey to Hagerstown. Col. Lumpkin died at the Kee Mar Army Hospital in September and was buried at the Presbyterian church on South Potomac Street (now the Fundamental Baptist Church). When the cemetery was removed, his remains were taken to Washington Confederate Cemetery. His is one of the very few individually marked graves at the Confederate cemetery. (Richard Clem.)

Lt. Isaac Burgauer, 3rd Arkansas Infantry, was wounded at Gettysburg and transported to Hagerstown. When he died on July 18, his last request was that he be buried in a Jewish cemetery in accordance with Jewish custom. The Israelite Benevolent Society of Hagerstown collected funds to have his remains prepared and taken to the Jewish cemetery in Chambersburg. Levi Stone transported the rebel lieutenant in his carriage to his final resting place in Pennsylvania. (Jim Wolfson.)

Van Wilson was a resident of Fayette County, Alabama, at the outbreak of the war. He enlisted in the Sumter Light Guards, a cavalry company that later mustered into Mississippi state service and became Company D of the Jeff Davis Legion. His brother served in an Alabama infantry regiment and died in the service of the Confederacy in the Peninsula Campaign of 1862. Van survived the carnage at Gettysburg only to be killed in action in Hagerstown during the retreat toward the Potomac. (Frances L. Brasher.)

Cpl. Lawrence Feigenschuh served in the 18th Pennsylvania Cavalry and was captured by the Confederates in Hagerstown on July 6. His company was involved in the repeated charges up Potomac Street. Feigenschuh was held as a prisoner of war until swapped in an 1864 prisoner exchange. (Robert Figenshu.)

First Lt. Gilbert Steward (left) poses here in a very rare image with an unidentified woman dressed in a man's uniform. Steward served in Company G, 1st Vermont Cavalry. He was wounded in the chest in the July 6 Battle of Hagerstown but recovered. (USAMHI.)

Pvt. Joseph E. Brewer served in Company B, 1st Vermont Cavalry. He was captured in the Battle of Hagerstown and was held at the Belle Isle prisoner-of-war camp, located on an island in the James River outside of Richmond. Private Brewer died of an unspecified illness at the prison camp on October 20, 1863, 14 weeks after his capture. (USAMHI.)

Brattleboro native Capt. Robert Schofield Jr. commanded Company F, 1st Vermont Cavalry. He was captured in the savage house-to-house fight in the streets and yards of Hagerstown in early July. Schofield mustered out as major of the regiment and lived in Wisconsin after the war. (USAMHI–Civil War Library and Museum, Philadelphia.)

Pvt. Dorence Atwater of the 2nd New York Cavalry was captured near Hagerstown on July 7 while carrying dispatches for General Kilpatrick. He was sent to Camp Sumter in Andersonville, Georgia, and assigned to the camp hospital. His job was to keep a record of all deaths that occurred. He kept the official Confederate record and maintained a second secret copy for himself. The official copy disappeared at war's end; but using his own copy, Atwater teamed with Clara Barton and ensured that 13,000 deceased prisoners' graves were individually marked. Due to his efforts, thousands of American soldiers do not lie in graves marked "unknown U.S. soldier." (USAMHI–Massachusetts Commandery, MOLLUS Collection.)

The Hager Mill on Mill Street is believed to be the scene of a July 6 encounter between troopers of the 11th Virginia Cavalry and a young girl with southern affection. She was wearing an apron in the red and white colors of rebel sympathy and was cheered by the soldiers as they passed. The girl gave the apron to Capt. Edward McDonald, whose command used it as a flag for the rest of the day. The "apron flag" became a noted sentimental artifact of the Southern cause, and an 1887 poem popularized the story. (Library of Congress.)

This replica of the historic apron flag was produced based on a photograph of the original in an old book. A Private Watkins of Romney, West Virginia, was mortally wounded near Jones' Crossroads late on the July 6 carrying the apron flag in battle. The location of the original apron, if it still exists, is not known. (Author's collection.)

Kee Mar College was again pressed into service by the Confederates as a hospital. Local doctors helped the Confederate medical staff tend to the hundreds of wounded arriving from Gettysburg and fresh Union and Confederate wounds inflicted in the battle in town. (WCHS.)

From July 6 until the Confederate withdrawal across the Potomac, the area between Hagerstown and Williamsport was a no-man's-land between entrenched armies. Here newspaper artist Edwin Forbes depicts a Union observation post in the attic of a house in Hagerstown's southern suburbs. The feet of a second observer can be seen near the top as he sits in a hatch or hole in the roof. (Library of Congress.)

When the Confederates evacuated Hagerstown, the wounded were entrusted to the care of such local doctors as John Absalom Wroe (pictured far right in the first row with his parents and siblings). Wroe must have felt many conflicting emotions dealing with the wounded Confederates. He was a native of the Commonwealth of Virginia. (Susan Howe.)

Dr. John A. Wroe lived on South Prospect Street. His residence, pictured here, stands today and is the home of the Hagerstown Women's Club. Dr. Wroe hosted Gen. Robert E. Lee and his staff for dinner one evening during the retreat from Gettysburg. (Susan Howe.)

The unrepentant southern sympathizer Dr. Charles MacGill opened a hospital for sick and wounded rebels in Hagerstown. When Lee's army retreated into Virginia, MacGill went with them and was commissioned a surgeon in the Confederate Medical Corps. He served in the hospitals around Richmond. His son, Charles G. W. MacGill, went to Gettysburg with Lee's army. The younger MacGill also went south with his father and received a commission as assistant surgeon in the 2nd Virginia Infantry of the famed Stonewall Brigade. (Frederick D. Shroyer.)

PENNSYLVANIA MILITIA LEAVING HAGERSTOWN, MARYLAND.

The Pennsylvania Militia occupied the Hagerstown area as the Union army chased the Confederates into Virginia. This image of South Potomac Street as seen from Public Square appeared in the *New York Illustrated News* in the weeks after the Battle of Hagerstown. (Ted Alexander.)

The buildings on the east side of the square in this *c.* 1890s image appear much as they did during the great street battle—although with some modifications. Today the Alexander House occupies the site of the buildings in the center and left of this image. (WCHS.)

Time marches on for all things, and signs of change are everywhere. Here this 1890s photograph of the building on the northwest corner of Franklin and Potomac Streets shows that it was enlarged in the years after the war from a two-story building with a gable roof to a three-story flat-roofed structure. The rebuilt Junior Fire Company is at right. The area in the foreground is the site of Captain Dahlgren's wounding during the battle, when he turned to the west upon discovering Confederates on West Franklin Street. (*Maryland Cracker Barrel.*)

Another building that witnessed the Civil War is the Hoover House, now known as the Patterson Building. Located across Franklin Street from city hall, it was a popular hotel. On April 1, 1865, Joseph Hoover purchased the property from the estate of Agnes Finegan, but it is possible that he operated Hoover House as a tenant before he purchased it. (*Maryland Cracker Barrel.*)

On July 12, Edwin Forbes, a correspondent/artist for *Frank Leslie's Illustrated Weekly*, sketched Union troops crossing the Antietam "at Funkstown," although it appears to be the Stull Mill at Mount Aetna Road's crossing of Antietam Creek, with some artistic liberties. The sketch was sent by express to Leslie's offices, where engravers transformed it into the woodcut seen below. The woodcut appeared in the August 1 issue of the magazine. (Above, Library of Congress; below, Tim Snyder.)

THE INVASION OF MARYLAND—GENERAL MEADE'S ARMY CROSSING THE ANTIETAM IN PURSUIT OF LEE, JULY 12TH, 1863.

Four

RANSOM, REDEMPTION, PEACE, AND TRAGEDY

1864–1865

As warring armies fought within miles and while troops regularly marched through and occupied Hagerstown, life went on for the local citizenry. Here several Hagerstown men lounge outside of Ullrich's Tobacco Store in 1864. Ullrich's was located on the south side of West Washington Street between today's Washington County Historical Society and the Discovery Station. Instead of the usual cigar store Indian, an African caricature is used in front of the shop. (WCHS.)

This photograph from around 1900 depicts a row of houses on the south side of East North Avenue, just east of North Potomac Street. The steeple of St. Paul's (now Otterbein United Methodist) Church on East Franklin Street is in the right background. Many of Hagerstown's Civil War–era homes have disappeared, including these, but they represent the working-class housing stock that existed in Hagerstown during the Civil War. (WCHS.)

On July 6, 1864, exactly one year after the Battle of Hagerstown, a 1,500-man cavalry brigade under Brig. Gen. John McCausland (left) came to Hagerstown. They were part of a small army under Gen. Jubal Early that had invaded Maryland to draw Union forces away from Lee's beleaguered army outside of Richmond. McCausland came with orders from Early to demand a ransom from the citizens to prevent the burning of the city in retaliation for scorched-earth tactics employed by Generals Hunter and Sheridan in the Shenandoah Valley. (West Virginia State Archives.)

McCausland established his headquarters in the town hall and met with city treasurer Matthew Barber (right) and the teller of the Hagerstown Bank, John Kausler (below). McCausland presented a written demand for $20,000 and 1,500 complete sets of men's clothing, with a deadline of three hours to produce all the funds and materials in the written demand. Barber and Kausler argued with the general that the expectations were impossible to meet on such short notice, but there was no negotiation. (Author's collection.)

John Kausler was employed in various positions by the Hagerstown Bank from the 1850s until the 1890s—first as teller, then bookkeeper, and finally as cashier. This photograph was taken late in his life, years after the war. (Author's collection.)

McCausland's demand was photographed by Bascom Phreaner in 1869. McCausland exacted $20,000 from the city plus 1,500 complete sets of clothing, a number corresponding with the number of men in his command. (Author's collection.)

Barber and Kausler turned to James Dixon Roman, president of the Hagerstown Bank and a former congressman during the Mexican War. Hobbled by a spinal illness, he could not walk to town hall from his home on West Washington Street. McCausland met him at the county courthouse. A stern discussion commenced in which Roman made it clear that they would find the funds but that it was entirely impossible for a town of 4,500 to secure 1,500 complete sets of clothing in three hours. (City of Hagerstown.)

Located west of Public Square, the Hagerstown Bank (left) was the heart of the city's financial industry. Roman arranged for his bank and two others to provide the cash ransom. The building was demolished in 1937 for a Montgomery Ward department store, which is now an office building for the Washington County government. The bank's successor in 2010 is the Hagerstown Trust Division of The Columbia Bank. The Updegraff buildings to the right still stand. (*Maryland Cracker Barrel.*)

Former congressman and Hagerstown Bank officer William T. Hamilton met McCausland and Roman at the courthouse. He strongly argued the lack of reason in requiring 1,500 sets of clothing in three hours from a town the size of Hagerstown. McCausland relented, demanding all the clothing that could be rounded up in three hours, with the understanding that Roman, Hamilton, and Kausler would keep the arrangement a secret from the citizens, so as to not encourage holding out or a slow response. As far as the citizenry knew, they had to produce 1,500 sets of clothing to save Hagerstown from the torch. (U.S. Senate Historical Office.)

Clerk of the circuit court Isaac Nesbitt was also engaged in the heated debate at the courthouse. After a settlement had been reached, McCausland, being in a hurry to rejoin Early's army, required Nesbitt to give his personal bond assuring that he would arrange for the destruction of the government's stores of war material at the Franklin Railroad's Walnut Street depot. His son, Alexander, was a captain in the 1st Maryland Cavalry (Union) and died in 1863. (WCHS.)

THE REBELS ROBBING THE FLOUR MILLS IN MARYLAND.

The grind of war resulted in the Confederates' conduct deteriorating from the largely respectful presence they exhibited during the two previous invasions. In the July 30, 1864, issue of *Harper's Weekly*, rebel quartermasters are shown commandeering the contents of Andrew Hager's Mill on Mill Street. (Tim Snyder.)

THE REBELS PILLAGING AT THE HAGERSTOWN DEPOT.

The Confederates also took as much from the army depot on Walnut Street as they could before it was burned. This image, looking south on Walnut from Franklin Street towards Washington, shows the back of St. Mary's Church on the left. This image also appeared in the July 30 issue of *Harper's Weekly*. (Tim Snyder.)

Those stores that were not cleaned out to meet McCausland's demand were treated roughly by Confederate soldiers, who paid for their "purchases" in Confederate money, which had no value in the North. Many small businesses were affected by Early's Raid. This c. 1880 photograph shows the common appearance of storefronts in Hagerstown during the war. (WCHS.)

Although the city market canopy did not exist during the Civil War, this c. 1890s photograph of the intersection of Franklin and North Potomac Streets shows it much as it was when McCausland made the town hall his headquarters in July 1864. (*Maryland Cracker Barrel*.)

The town of Hagerstown, having com-
plied with the foregoing requisition
by paying in cash the sum of Twenty
Thousand dollars ($20 000) & having
also furnished the supplies called
to a value of [illegible]
their commutation I hereby certify
to the fact, & leave the town under
the protection of the confederate
forces, relieving the citizens & their
property from further contribution
& agreeing to shield both from further
requirements.

Genl. McCausland
Bg Genl. C. S. A.

Coats — 243
Pants 203
Drawers 132
Hose 437
Boots 97
Shoes 123
Hats 830
Shirts 225
Pc. Goods 1370½ 7 ds.
Clothing assorted

To confirm compliance and secure the town from further demands, General McCausland provided
the city with a receipt for the ransom. Included in that acknowledgment was an inventory of the
clothing that was collected in the allotted three-hour period. (Author's collection.)

Col. Henry A. Cole of Frederick (left) commanded a regiment of Maryland cavalry. On July 29, his troops battled a brigade of Confederate cavalry for three hours until they were compelled to retreat toward Greencastle. The force he opposed was commanded by Brig. Gen. John Crawford Vaughn of Tennessee. (USAMHI.)

After pushing Colonel Cole's men out of the city, Vaughn's forces entered the Franklin Railroad yards on the west side of the town and destroyed as much of the railroad equipment and stockpiled supplies as they could in the limited amount of time they had to work. Vaughn's force circled through the area again on August 5 and engaged in what would become the last Confederate occupation of Hagerstown. (USAMHI–Massachusetts Commandery, MOLLUS Collection.)

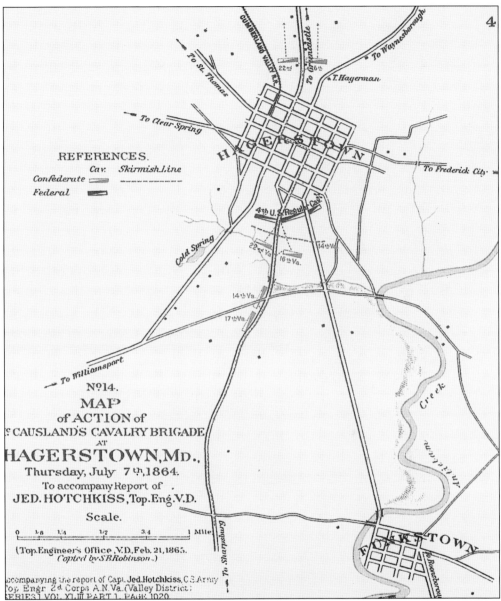

The topographical engineers (mapmakers) of both the Union and Confederate armies left fairly detailed records of the actions in local areas. General Meade's engineers produced maps showing the trenches created between Hagerstown and Williamsport in 1863 that can be compared against modern maps to identify approximate locations of the positions both armies held. Here Jedediah Hotchkiss, the mapmaker attached to Early's army, filed a report containing this map accurately showing Hagerstown's street layout at that time and the positions of Union and Confederate cavalry involved in a skirmish on the edge of town in late July. (Author's collection.)

South Prospect Street was developed in the 1830s and 1840s. The house in the right background is located where North Prospect Street lies today. Beyond the fence in the center is the Rochester House. Both homes on the left in this *c.* 1870s photograph still stand. (WCHS.)

This postwar image depicts the 100 block of West Washington Street as it would have appeared during the Civil War. The building that now houses the Washington County Historical Society is on the far left. The photograph was taken in front of the home of Dr. Augustine Mason, who commanded the Confederate military hospitals in Richmond from 1863 until the end of the war. (WCHS.)

J. H. Beachley's Dry Goods Store was located on the northeast corner of Public Square. This photograph appears to date to around 1870. The street to the right is East Washington Street. This streetscape, with the storefront, corniced buildings, and structures with sloped roofs and dormers is very characteristic of the city center area of Hagerstown during the mid-19th century. Beachley's Dry Goods Store survives to this day as the Beachley Furniture Company. (*Maryland Cracker Barrel.*)

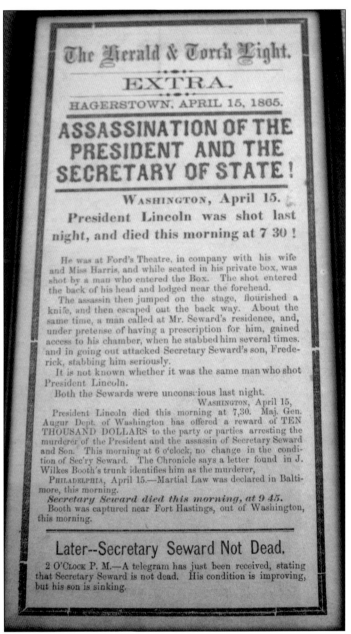

The Herald & Torch Light.

EXTRA.

HAGERSTOWN, APRIL 15, 1865.

ASSASSINATION OF THE PRESIDENT AND THE SECRETARY OF STATE!

WASHINGTON, April 15.

President Lincoln was shot last night, and died this morning at 7 30 !

He was at Ford's Theatre, in company with his wife and Miss Harris, and while seated in his private box, was shot by a man who entered the Box. The shot entered the back of his head and lodged near the forehead.

The assassin then jumped on the stage, flourished a knife, and then escaped out the back way. About the same time, a man called at Mr. Seward's residence, and, under pretense of having a prescription for him, gained access to his chamber, when he stabbed him several times, and in going out attacked Secretary Seward's son, Frederick, stabbing him seriously.

It is not known whether it was the same man who shot President Lincoln.

Both the Sewards were unconscious last night.

WASHINGTON, April 15,

President Lincoln died this morning at 7,30. Maj. Gen. Augur Dept. of Washington has offered a reward of TEN THOUSAND DOLLARS to the party or parties arresting the murderer of the President and the assassin of Secretary Seward and Son. This morning at 6 o'clock, no change in the condition of Sec'ry Seward. The Chronicle says a letter found in J. Wilkes Booth's trunk identifies him as the murderer,

PHILADELPHIA, April 15.—Martial Law was declared in Baltimore, this morning.

Secretary Seward died this morning, at 9 45.

Booth was captured near Fort Hastings, out of Washington, this morning.

Later--Secretary Seward Not Dead.

2 O'CLOCK P. M.—A telegram has just been received, stating that Secretary Seward is not dead. His condition is improving, but his son is sinking.

In early April 1865, word came from the hamlet of Appomattox Courthouse in Virginia that the Army of Northern Virginia had finally been compelled to surrender to Union forces. When this news reached Hagerstown, civic celebrations were held by the pro-Union majority in the community, while those who supported the vanquished Confederacy quietly mourned the loss. Less than a week later, joy turned to shock and sorrow on the parts of almost all residents, regardless of their sympathies in the war, when word was received that President Lincoln had been assassinated. Businesses closed, public buildings were draped in black, and churches conducted memorial services. This handbill, photographed in an exhibit at the Washington County Museum of Fine Arts, was published by the *Herald and Torchlight* to spread information as quickly as possible about the calamity that had befallen the nation. (WMR-WCFL.)

Five

RECOVERY, REUNION, AND REMEMBRANCE
HAGERSTOWN AFTER THE WAR

In 1888, supporters of Benjamin Harrison's presidential campaign picked up on the "Keep the Ball Rolling" slogan of his grandfather's 1840 campaign for president. A large ball was rolled from his home in North Bend, Ohio, to Washington, D.C. This publicity stunt was photographed on West Washington Street, facing east toward Public Square, from the balcony of the Baldwin House Hotel (at the location of the former Washington House Hotel). The Hagerstown Bank is on the right of the photograph. Harrison was a general in the Union Army during the war. Veterans organizations, both in the North and the South, played major influential roles in the outcome of elections in the late 19th century. (WCHS.)

Amos W. Brandenberg enlisted in the 6th Maryland Infantry in 1862. In the waning days of the war, he was wounded in the foot. Amputation was required, and he was discharged for disability and sent home to resume his life. The wound did not heal properly, and Brandenberg died of complications at his family's farm on the Leitersburg Pike within weeks. In 2006, Brandenberg's silver corps badge was found on the farm. Whether it was lost or discarded there is unknown. (Dennis Easterday.)

A corps badge was a cloth ornament in a shape assigned to each army corps and color-coded for each division within the corps. The first three divisions were designated, in order, red, white, and blue. The Swiss cross designated the 6th Corps. The recessed area in the middle likely contained blue enamel, corresponding to the regiment's place in the 3rd Division. Brandenberg's privately purchased silver badge, inscribed with his name, doubled as a makeshift dog tag. (Dennis Easterday.)

U. S. SENATORS, 43d CONGRESS.

In 1868, former congressman William Thomas Hamilton was elected to the U.S. Senate. He served one term and was later elected the 38th governor of Maryland, leading the state from 1880 to 1884. Here, he is pictured (third row, fourth from right) with his fellow U.S. senators on the east front of the Capitol on February 12, 1874. Many Civil War politicians and generals are featured, including Confederate major general John B. Gordon of Georgia (first row, far left), who was wounded in the face at the Battle of Antietam, Sen. John Sherman of Ohio (third row, fifth from right), who authored the Sherman Anti-Trust Act, and former Confederate general Matt Ransom of North Carolina (third row, sixth from right). Also pictured are Sen. Simon Cameron of Pennsylvania (first row, fourth from left), who was President Lincoln's secretary of war at the beginning of the Civil War, and Sen. Zachariah Chandler of Michigan (first row, fourth from right), who was a major senate critic of President Lincoln's during the war. Sen. John A. Logan of Illinois (third row, second from right) was a major general in the Union army and, as commander of the Grand Army of the Republic, was primarily responsible for the creation of Memorial Day. (U.S. Senate Historical Office.)

The tradition of Decoration Day began almost before the Civil War ended, when citizens in the North and the South would visit soldier graveyards and local cemeteries to decorate the graves of the fallen with floral tributes. In 1868, Gen. John A. Logan, national commander of the Grand Army of the Republic, issued an order to all GAR posts to observe an official Decoration Day on May 30 of that year. This appears to be the first semblance of an official commemoration. The holiday is now known as Memorial Day. Southern states ultimately adopted varying dates, typically in June, to honor the Confederacy's fallen soldiers. The movement grew quickly, with regular observances started all across the country. Here the children of nearby Leitersburg pose for a photograph in the town square as part of an observance around World War I. By this time, half a century had passed, and the ranks of the blue and the gray were rapidly fading away. (Dorothy Smith.)

After building a business as one of the preeminent studio photographers in Washington County, Elias Recher became fascinated by the stereopticon process, a forerunner of the GAF View-Master that has entertained many children in the 1950s. The process involved taking two simultaneous photographs, slightly apart, mounting them side-by-side on a card, then inserting the card into an adjustable viewer with two lenses to create a three-dimensional effect. Most stereographs were of landmarks and scenery and were intended for widespread commercial distribution. Recher's stereographic photographs of the Hagerstown GAR reunion of 1884 appear later in this chapter, and his stereo images of Antietam Battlefield, the dedication of Antietam National Cemetery, and recreational activities at Pen Mar Park near Cascade enjoyed wide distribution. In this photograph, Elias and a young helper appear in one of Recher's own stereographic cards. (WCHS.)

Joshua Thomas served during the war as a musician in the 12th Maryland Infantry Regiment and later joined Reno Post No. 4, Grand Army of the Republic. He is shown here in his GAR uniform. Thomas served as one of several delegates representing posts in the state of Maryland at the annual GAR National Encampment in September 1915, which was held in Washington, D.C. Aside from his Civil War service, Thomas has the unique place in history of being the operator of the first bookmobile in the United States. (WMR-WCFL.)

The Washington County Free Library initiated the first bookmobile in the country in 1905. The purpose was to extend the library's reach to people in the far-flung rural corners of the county. By 1904, sixty-six "book stations" containing 30 volumes each were established throughout the county's general stores and post offices. The bookmobile was then created to refresh the materials at these stations and provided mobile service. The task of running the bookmobile fell to Joshua Thomas, the library's janitor. He operated the bookmobile from 1905 until August 25, 1910, when the wagon was struck by a Norfolk and Western train at St. James. Thomas was thrown from the wagon and received moderate injuries. The horses bolted but were uninjured. The wagon was destroyed, but many books were salvaged from the wreckage. Here, Thomas is shown at right at Grimm's Blacksmith Shop in Cearfoss. (WMR-WCFL.)

The men of the Western Enterprise Fire Company turn out in front of their station on West Franklin Street, east of McPherson Street, around 1890. Undoubtedly some of these men were Civil War veterans, and their uniforms and formation show the influence of the Civil War military on postwar fire companies. The elderly gentleman in the front right appears to be wearing a GAR membership medal. The Western Enterprise Fire Company later moved to a new building on Washington Square. This structure stood where the CSX railroad overpass crosses West Franklin Street, one-half block east of North Burhans Boulevard. (Western Enterprise Fire Company.)

Comdr. Donald Fairfax served 44 years in the navy, including service in the Mexican War. In 1861, he was the executive officer of the USS *San Jacinto*. On November 8, Capt. Charles Wilkes ordered that the British mail ship *Trent* be stopped in international waters and searched for two Confederate emissaries bound for Europe; the orders were carried out by Fairfax. He found and arrested the diplomats. The Trent Affair was an international incident that almost led to war with Britain. Fairfax went on to command ironclad monitors in combat and was commandant of the U.S. Naval Academy from 1863 to 1865. A minor national celebrity from his Civil War service, he retired as a rear admiral in 1881. Fairfax moved to Hagerstown, where he lived at 163 South Prospect Street until his passing in 1894. (Author's collection.)

In 1860, Fairfax served as executive officer of USS *Constellation* (now a museum in Baltimore) on the west coast of Africa. *Constellation*'s mission was to capture slave ships running human cargo to the western hemisphere. On September 26, it captured the barque *Cora* and liberated 705 Africans. *Constellation* repatriated the captives at Monrovia, Liberia, and its crewmen took *Cora* to New York for disposition in a "prize court." (Author's collection.)

Clear Spring native Edward Kershner received a commission as an assistant surgeon in the U.S. Navy in the fall of 1861 and reported for duty aboard USS *Cumberland* at Hampton Roads, Virginia. On March 6, 1862, the ironclad CSS *Virginia* (also known as the *Merrimack*) steamed into Hampton Roads and laid waste to the Union's wooden warships. After tending to the wounded, Kershner was one of the last two men to dive from *Cumberland* before she went to the bottom. He later served aboard several ironclad warships and retired from the navy in 1902. Kershner lived on the west side of Oak Hill Avenue where it meets Potomac Avenue. The home was demolished in the 1940s. (WCHS.)

John Henry Murphy was born a slave in Baltimore. Freed in 1863, he enlisted in Company G, 30th United States Colored Troops and rose to the rank of sergeant. After the war, Murphy held a number of positions, including district superintendent of Sunday schools for the Hagerstown area A.M.E. churches. In 1896, he purchased the *Baltimore Afro-American* newspaper and, over 26 years, built it into the premier African-American newspaper of the 20th century. It is still published in 2010. During World War II, Sergeant Murphy received the honor of a Liberty Ship being named for him. (*Baltimore Afro-American.*)

After the war, Hagerstonians returned to pick up the pieces of their lives and moved on. This led to what would be the greatest period of growth and expansion in city history in the later 19th century. Here the storefront of Middle States Building and Loan, located on West Washington Street, lists many of Hagerstown's prominent Civil War citizens as its officers and a former Confederate officer as its corporate attorney. (WMR-WCFL.)

The *Morning Herald* and the *Herald and Torchlight* were the city's two prominent newspapers during and after the Civil War. Here the staff poses outside of the Summit Avenue offices around 1890. Today Hagerstown's daily newspaper combines the names of two Civil War era firms for its masthead, the *Herald-Mail*. (WMR-WCFL.)

Ira Hayes spent his early youth (including the Civil War period) in Wolfsville. Shortly after the war, his family moved to Hagerstown and opened a store. Young Ira became a printer's devil at the *Twice A Week* newspaper. The *Twice A Week's* offices were located on the northwest corner of Public Square (see cover photograph). A printer's devil is a trade term for a youthful apprentice who would run errands and deliveries, typeset basic copy, and generally learn the trade. Ira enjoyed a long career in the local press. He is shown here, around 1868, in the attire and with the tools of his trade. (WCHS.)

Henry Kyd Douglas taught at the Hagerstown Academy before joining the Confederate army. He returned to Hagerstown to open a law practice in 1867. In 1862, Douglas was the youngest officer on the staff of Gen. Thomas J. "Stonewall" Jackson. Rising through the officer corps, he later commanded a brigade at the Confederate surrender at Appomattox, Virginia. Douglas served as a judge on the circuit court of Washington County, ran unsuccessfully for Congress, and served many years in the Maryland National Guard, where he rose to the rank of major general. He is shown here in his major general's uniform. Douglas served as adjutant general of the Maryland National Guard during the administration of Gov. Frank Brown (1892–1896). Altered in appearance, the home he owned from 1878 until his death in 1903 stands today at 405 North Potomac Street. His diaries and postwar recollections served as the basis of the book *I Rode With Stonewall*, published in 1940 by his nephew John Beckenbaugh. (WMR-WCFL.)

In 1884, Douglas arranged to have Stonewall Jackson's favorite war horse, Fancy, brought to Hagerstown for the Washington County Agricultural Fair. Commonly known as Little Sorrel, the horse was a sensation. It is said that his tail and mane were plucked nearly clean by souvenir hunters. Fancy was photographed at Douglas's home on North Potomac Street, held by Napoleon Bonaparte Hull Sr., an 84-year-old veteran of the 14th Virginia Cavalry who lived on nearby East Bethel Street (Randolph Avenue). (Author's collection.)

With war's end, the men of the MacGill family were eager to resume their lives. The senior Dr. MacGill and several of his children moved to Richmond, Virginia. The junior Dr. MacGill relocated to Catonsville, Maryland. James MacGill (pictured) served in Company C, 1st Maryland Cavalry. He moved to Pulaski, Virginia, and married the niece of Gen. J. E. B. Stuart. James later married Lucy Lee Hill, daughter of Gen. A. P. Hill and goddaughter of Gen. Robert E. Lee. James went on to serve as the commander of the Virginia Division of the United Confederate Veterans and is pictured here in his veterans' association uniform. (Author's collection.)

The Grand Army of the Republic was a Union veterans's organization formed in 1866. Local posts served as social and memorial organizations as well as serving as charities to help their members who had fallen on hard times. The Gen. Jesse Lee Reno Post was formed in Hagerstown between 1866 and 1868. It was the fourth post organized in Maryland. The nearest camps of the Confederate equivalent, the United Confederate Veterans, were in Frederick and Shepherdstown. This Reno Post membership badge was owned by Comrade George W. Frush. (Daniel C. Toomey Collection.)

Clear Spring area resident George W. Frush wears the badge shown in the photograph above. Frush enlisted in the 1st Maryland Potomac Home Brigade Infantry Regiment in September 1861. He was captured at Duffields, West Virginia, on June 28, 1864, but returned to service. When the war ended, Frush was serving as a sergeant in the 13th Maryland Infantry. (Daniel C. Toomey Collection.)

On April 1, 1905, Reno Post No. 4, GAR signed a lease with the city to use a lodge room on the third floor of Hagerstown City Hall. This room had previously been leased to Masonic and Odd Fellows lodges. Reno Post met twice a month on the first and third Wednesdays of the month. The room was decorated with relics of the Civil War. A second post, Lyon Post No. 31, was home to Hagerstown's African American Union veterans. They convened on the first and third Thursdays of the month. Their meeting location is not known. (WMR-WCFL.)

An unidentified member of Reno Post No. 4 attends a ceremony at the Tomb of the Unknown Soldier in 1922. In 1921, America selected one unidentified soldier to represent thousands who perished in World War I, to be joined later by soldiers from future wars. (WMR-WCFL.)

Henry F. Roberts was born into slavery in Hagerstown. After securing his freedom, he moved to Oswego County, New York. When the Union army began recruiting African American soldiers, he enlisted in Company F, 29th Connecticut Volunteer Infantry (Colored) and attained the rank of corporal. He returned to Oswego County at the conclusion of the war. Being that he was likely the only African American veteran in his part of Oswego County, Roberts was accepted for membership by the all-white Barney Post of the GAR at Sandy Creek, New York. Roberts is seen here proudly wearing his Barney Post GAR ribbons. For several years, he served as color bearer of the post. (Town of Sandy Creek, New York.)

The 29th Connecticut Volunteer Infantry appears on dress parade in Beaufort, South Carolina. Corporal Roberts would have been among this formation of troops. (Library of Congress.)

In 1884, the Maryland GAR held its annual encampment in Hagerstown at the Agricultural Fairgrounds. In this Elias Recher stereograph, GAR members are amused by a boy riding an "elephant" (two national guardsmen covered with an army blanket). On a national level, the GAR was a potent political force, and this likely involves some inference to the Republican Party—whether it is positive or negative is undetermined. (Michael Pekosky.)

Elias Recher also captured this image of the Maryland Grand Army of the Republic members and members of the Maryland and Virginia National Guard as they form a dress parade at the Hagerstown encampment. (Daniel C. Toomey Collection.)

Hagerstonian George Freaner "went South" and attained the rank of major on the staffs of generals J. E. B. Stuart, Wade Hampton, and Fitzhugh Lee. Returning home, Freaner formed a law firm with Andrew Syester that quickly became one of the most prominent firms in the county. Freaner also served with Colonel Douglas on the commission that created Washington Confederate Cemetery. When the cemetery was dedicated in 1874, Freaner hosted the keynote speaker (his former boss), Gen. Fitzhugh Lee, at his Summit Avenue home. Freaner married and fathered two daughters—Lucy (right) in 1874 and Jessie (below) in 1873. These photographs appear to have been taken around 1877. Soon after the completion of the cemetery, Freaner's health began to fail. Although in poor health, his death in 1878 at age 47 came as somewhat of a surprise to all who knew him. (WCHS.)

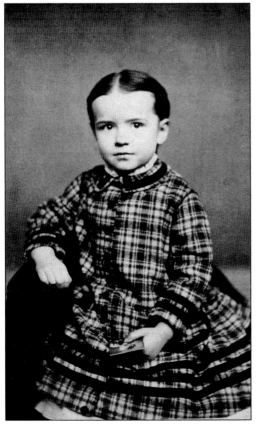

Jerome M. Lawrence served in Company G, 165th Pennsylvania Volunteer Infantry, a nine-month regiment that served from November 9, 1862, until the end of July 1863. Company G was recruited in Adams County, Pennsylvania. The 165th managed to miss large battles but was involved in skirmishes in the area east of Richmond. After the Civil War, Lawrence settled in Hagerstown and became a member of St. Mary's Catholic Church. He resided at 411 Jefferson Street in his twilight years. When he passed away at his home at age 90 on October 14, 1930, he was one of the very last surviving Civil War veterans in the Hagerstown area. This image was shared through the courtesy of his descendants. (Lt. Margaret Kline, retired, Hagerstown Police Department.)

The first real test of a reunited America came when war was declared on Spain in 1898. Veterans of the blue and gray sent their sons off to fight side by side. To encourage southern support for the Spanish-American War, Washington gave former high-ranking Confederates commissions as generals and appointments to other important posts in the U.S. Volunteers. Hagerstown's Colonel Douglas was offered a staff major's commission, but he declined the post due to health concerns and dissatisfaction with the post offered. Here the boys of Hagerstown's Company B, 1st Maryland Volunteers celebrate at Camp MacKenzie, Georgia, on February 1, 1899, upon learning that they are to be mustered out. The 1st Regiment was commanded by Hagerstonian colonel William Preston Lane Sr., father of future Maryland governor William P. Lane Jr. Pictured from left to right are (first row) Pvt. Thomas H. Spielman, Cpl. Jacob Herman Reichard, Pvt. Charles E. Fry, and Charles A. Rothweil; (second row) Cpl. George B. Alexander, Sgt. Marshall J. Beachtell, and Pvt. James H. Harley; (third row) Cpl. Richard Duffy and Cpl. Murphy E. Flory. Alone in the top row is Hospital Steward Herbert Kneisley. (WCHS.)

In September 1937, the city hosted *On Wings of Time*, a large fair and pageant detailing the history of the county. It was held to commemorate the 75th anniversary of the Battle of Antietam. Historic railroad engines were brought into the fairgrounds via a temporary rail spur (shown on the right edge of this image). Stages were constructed on the infield for viewing by the public, seated in the grandstands (upper right). (WMR-WCFL.)

Some of the pageant's cast poses for a group photograph in front of the set. The scale and scope of this project is quite impressive considering that it occurred at the height of the Great Depression. Advertisements and promotional literature boasted of a cast of 1,500 and a stage 600 feet wide, stating that it would be the "largest show in the east this year." (WCHS.)

Over time, many of Hagerstown's 19th-century landmarks fell to the wrecker's ball as the city center grew and properties redeveloped. On June 29, 1959, Ruth Davis and her daughter Julie Ann (now Julie Hayslett) watch former governor William T. Hamilton's home being demolished. Hamilton's house, located on the north side of the 200 block of West Washington Street, was originally constructed as the Valley Bank. Hamilton purchased the bank building in the 1850s for conversion to a residence. Its place was taken by an expansion of the St. Mary's parochial school. The contract for demolition was awarded to the C. William Hetzer Construction Company. Established in 1955, Hetzer Construction is headquartered near Hagerstown. (WMR-WCFL, Vernon Davis Collection.)

The 4th Maryland Artillery, CSA, was a locally based reenactment unit that served during the Civil War centennial in the late 1950s and early 1960s. Armed with an original 12-pounder "Napoleon" pulled by a team of mules, the cannoneers draw their gun down North Potomac Street into Public Square during the 1959 Veterans Day Parade. (WMR-WCFL, Vernon Davis Collection.)

On September 3, 1961, Hagerstown hosted former president Dwight Eisenhower, who traveled from his farm near Gettysburg to speak at the rededication of the Washington Confederate Cemetery. With him was Gen. U. S. Grant III, grandson of the Union general and president and chairman of the Civil War Centennial Commission from 1957 to July 1961. (WMR-WCFL.)

From 2008 to 2010, the City of Hagerstown secured grants from the Maryland Heritage Area program to install 50 Civil War history interpretive panels in the city center and surrounding neighborhoods. Many of the stories and illustrations found in this book are included in greater detail in the contents of these historic markers. (City of Hagerstown.)

www.arcadiapublishing.com

Discover books about the town where you grew up, the cities where your friends and families live, the town where your parents met, or even that retirement spot you've been dreaming about. Our Web site provides history lovers with exclusive deals, advanced notification about new titles, e-mail alerts of author events, and much more.

MADE IN THE USA

Arcadia Publishing, the leading local history publisher in the United States, is committed to making history accessible and meaningful through publishing books that celebrate and preserve the heritage of America's people and places. Consistent with our mission to preserve history on a local level, this book was printed in South Carolina on American-made paper and manufactured entirely in the United States.

This book carries the accredited Forest Stewardship Council (FSC) label and is printed on 100 percent FSC-certified paper. Products carrying the FSC label are independently certified to assure consumers that they come from forests that are managed to meet the social, economic, and ecological needs of present and future generations.

FSC
Mixed Sources
Product group from well-managed forests and other controlled sources

Cert no. SW-COC-001530
www.fsc.org
© 1996 Forest Stewardship Council

Find *Your* Place in History.